D1179954

GP 10³

J. L. McAnaney
6128 Kantor Street
San Diego, Cal. 92122

The *Royal Oak* Courts Martial

THE *ROYAL OAK* COURTS MARTIAL

by

LESLIE GARDINER

This book is published and distributed
in the United States by the

UNITED STATES NAVAL INSTITUTE
Annapolis, Maryland 21402

WILLIAM BLACKWOOD & SONS LTD
EDINBURGH AND LONDON
1965

PRINTED IN GREAT BRITAIN BY
WILLIAM BLACKWOOD & SONS LTD., EDINBURGH

TO MY FATHER

Acknowledgments

I WISH to thank those old friends and former colleagues of the principal characters in the *Royal Oak* affair who generously responded to my appeal for information. They include: Mrs Joan Osborne, Mrs B. Foster, Mrs I. M. Willis, Captain Taprell Dorling, D.S.O., R.N. (Retd), Captain G. T. Coney, O.B.E., R.N. (Retd), Commander J. G. Hopkins, R.N. (Retd), Warrant Writer A. J. Saunders, R.N. (Retd), Mr P. E. Robinson, Mr W. Ellis, and ex-Bandmaster Percy Barnacle, R.M.

I am particularly obliged to the late Vice-Admiral K. G. B. Dewar and Mrs Dewar, to Mrs C. Powell and Mr John K. Daniel for courteously answering numerous questions; to Miss Ella Warren, Captain Lionel Dawson, R.N. (Retd), and Captain N. T. P. Cooper, C.B.E., R.N. (Retd), for news of Malta at the period with which this book deals; to Captain C. E. Keys, R.N. (Retd), for the loan of his Journal as a Midshipman in H.M.S. *Royal Oak*; and to Admiral Sir William James, G.C.B., for permission to quote from his book *The Sky was Always Blue*.

Extracts from *The Navy from Within* are included by permission of the author, the late Vice-Admiral K. G. B. Dewar, C.B.E.

LESLIE GARDINER

GIFFORD,
EAST LOTHIAN

Contents

Illustrations

The artist's impression of the Court Martial Scene is reproduced
by permission of Associated Newspapers Limited. The photograph of Sir Roger Keyes was supplied by the Illustrated London
News & Sketch Limited, and the frontispiece by Central Press
Photos Limited.

CHAPTER I

Sunrise at Malta

OVER Malta the dawn mists are rising. If you have arrived in Grand Harbour during the night and are early on deck for a first glimpse of the island, the sand-coloured ramparts of the citadel stand well-washed and empty for your inspection. It is not easy to see by what channel your ship got in or how she will get out again. You have sailed into a harbour that was dug out of the heart of an island metropolis, as a quarry is dug. On one side rises Valletta, stoutly corseted in line upon line of wall; on the other the thickly crowded tenements and palaces of the three cities, Senglea, Cospicua, Vittoriosa. Both sides grow out of the malleable yellow cliffs that enclose the inlets, both are decorated with a skyline of towers and belfries. Already, down from the heights, around the sprawling creeks, comes the tentative tolling of a bell or two. These are ranging shots that will develop into a prolonged barrage of strident tintinnabulation as the day wears on.

Sunrise on a spring morning finds Grand Harbour looking its best. A few dghaisas are abroad – beaky, archaic-style rowboats, a cross between Venetian gondola and miniature Viking galley. One is poling silently towards the Marina with a church party for early mass. The rest drift on tideless waters, as they have done all night, waiting for the ships to wake up. Brawny, sun-blackened, slab-faced dghaisa-

A   I

men snore in the stern-sheets, mongrel mixtures like their boats, relics of half the extinguished seafaring races of the Mediterranean. Later in the morning, when the reveillé cry of " Ao Dghaisa ! " goes up from ship and shore and floating dock, when returning libertymen congregate at Customs House steps, these boatmen will stand to their oars and breast-stroke towards their fares, uttering sharp, incomprehensible cries like seafowl converging on a windfall bucket of fish-heads. Between trips their time will be spent in sleep, in lying in ambush for tourists, or in touching up the gaudily ornamented prows and panels and name-plates of their boats with driblets of paint wheedled out of the chief bo'sun's mates of the fleet. The scrollwork and gold leaf on the dghaisas usually incorporates a fanciful representation of an admiral's flag or white ensign, and their names repeat the famous ship-names of long ago: *Thunderer, Iron Duke, Queen Elizabeth, Renown.*

About seventy years ago, when the first battleship's noisy brass-funnelled steam picket-boat churned past him in a cloud of black smoke, a dghaisaman screamed at it and shook his fists, prophesying the doom of Malta's ancient boat trade. He need not have worried. The dghaisas of today, anachronistic as ever, are as numerous as ever. It is the battleships and the picket-boats that have disappeared. And of the warships that remain, lavishly equipped as they are with all manner of fast small craft, from rakish one-man ' skimmer ' to superbly caparisoned admiral's barge, each ship still hires its own dghaisa on first arrival on the Mediterranean station and pays a retaining fee for it when absent on manoeuvres or on a cruise. And its owner still inhabits the *manderaggio* – the mediaeval slum-caves beneath Valletta – or else has no home at all apart from his boat; and is still suspected to be among Malta's richer citizens.

First the protective ring of ramparts, the yellow masonry, and then the dghaisas, littering creek and roadstead – this is how the characteristic sights of the island strike the new-comer who has arrived, as so many do, in Grand Harbour overnight. Third is the fleet. This has been the Mediter-ranean headquarters of the Royal Navy for a hundred years and more.

Down the middle of Grand Harbour run lines of buoys to which every naval captain periodically comes to have his reputation for ship-handling assessed under the eye of the Commander-in-Chief himself – his *belvedere* surveys them and his telescope is trained on them on most occasions when vessels leave or enter harbour. At these moorings the fleet has lain all night, silent and sleeping, but still wearing the air of instant readiness and immaculate tidiness that is exclusive to the Mediterranean squadrons. Now the sun is up and so, in each warship, are the duty watch and the men under punishment. The dew is not yet off the decks, guns are covered and awnings sloped against it. The first dghaisaman is just stirring, stretching and yawning, sending small ripples out from his motionless boat. Ashore, the first clop of wooden sandals is heard and the first solitary *faldetta* seen (a stiff black cowl like half a coracle, the tradi-tional feminine headgear of the island) bobbing up steep steps to a yellow-domed church. Faintly, from a side-street, comes the milkman's cry of " *Halib!* " His nanny-goat, trailing the half-on-half-off brassière that regulation requires her to wear, chews paper in the gutter – until the

clank of a tin-can let down from a window matches the
clank of her bell and both chime in with the *campanile* clank
from distant Senglea or Floriana. The last curtains of mist
are dissolving into hard blue sky and the day warms up to
the long summer drought – if this is March, only a shower
or two of rain can be expected in the next six months.

And already the Royal Navy's wash-deck hoses are rigged
and bare-footed seamen in night clothing (not pyjamas, but
a sailor suit without a collar) and trousers rolled above their
knees are brooming up and down industriously to the petty
officer's ritual chant of " Scrub forward . . . scrub aft ".
Duty electricians trot round, switching off illumination
circuits (woe betide the officer of the watch who has not got
this done and his anchor lights out within moments of morning twilight officially ending, *per* Nautical Almanac). A
stoker comes off watch, up through the manhole and straight
to the ship's side with a handful of cotton waste – and does
a smart about-turn at the sight of the duty lieutenant-
commander on his rounds. Malta's hot, narrow, dusty
streets may not be the tidiest, but at least the Royal Navy
keeps its waters clean. The milkman's goat would find little
to munch on the surface of Grand Harbour.

Subdued bugle-calls break out here and there; then a
chorus, more or less in unison, for the fleet acts as one unit
and the same general routine is observed by all; the cheerful
tum-ti-tum-ti of ' Call the Hands ', followed shortly by
' Cooks to the Galley ' and the pipes that launch the ship on
her working day again – ' Respread awnings ' . . . ' Un-
cover guns ' . . . ' Hands to breakfast and clean '.

Duty boats' crews are in their boats, scrubbing out.
Side-boys straddle the boom, from which buckets and

brushes depend on lengths of spunyarn. Quarter-deck gangways are being washed, dried and polished before traffic starts to move on them. With a sudden cough and the roar of a racing-car engine, one power-boat after another gets under way and heads for the Marina – perhaps to pick up a ' native ' first lieutenant with wife and family ashore, who is still expected to be on board for the first muster of the hands; or perhaps with a party of subordinate officers for the Marsa and a crack-of-dawn hockey or polo fixture. If the seaman rises early, the midshipman rises earlier.

These are the forerunners in a day-long procession of fast motor-boats. They join ship to shore and ship to ship with criss-crossing furrows of mathematical directness, perpetually rocking the dghaisas with their wash.

The British fleet at its moorings on the land-locked inlets within the fortress of Malta makes a spectacle to open the eyes of tourists in many a Mediterranean cruising liner or boat of passage. They have no idea the Navy ran so many ships. But Britain's main naval strength has long been deployed in these waters and a greater concentration of warships is to be seen here, even today, than almost anywhere in the world.

Malta is still a staging post on the India, Australia and Far Eastern routes. The sea that washes her rocks washes also the coasts of lands on whose frontiers conflicting aims have always met and still meet. A change in the status or policy of a Mediterranean country still upsets world equilibrium.

But the Malta-based fleet of today is a pitiable sight to the sailor who remembers the nineteen-twenties – to go no further back than that. He sees an aircraft-carrier, perhaps – just one, admittedly rather larger than anything that was afloat when he was at sea; a cruiser or two, with stumpy masts festooned in surrealist cages and networks of metal and no visible armament worth speaking of; a bare half-dozen destroyers – frigates, they call them now, he learns ; and that is the fleet, unless you include a few miscellaneous craft that he himself would not dignify with the name of warship, except that they wear the white ensign.

" They tell me I wouldn't recognise the place," says a retired bluejacket who doesn't get about a lot these days. They are right. Air-raid damage during the war made little difference to the topography. The islanders have not changed much either; they still cling obstinately and rather endearingly to habits that were well ingrained when St Paul was a sailor. But what gave Malta its brightest appearance, the scene that the word Malta evokes in the memories of sailors and soldiers and residents and travellers of forty years ago – this has gone, and gone for good. The days of the naval occupation are days of the past.

During the nineteen-twenties, Britain maintained in the Mediterranean what would nowadays be regarded as a vast fleet. Ashore in Malta, at no time of the day or night could one turn the head without seeing naval and marine uniforms. When the ships were present, their crews were everywhere ashore, seeming to outnumber an already swarming population. Ferries from Sicily, mail packets and ' Grey Funnel ' liners (navalese for troopships) were constantly edging in from England with cargoes of more soldiers and sailors, together with wives and families and those hopeful young women who came out to sample the social life of the island and were sometimes rather unkindly referred to as the ' fishing fleet '.

Cheap, exotic, lively, climatically desirable, a paradise in so many respects to people with widely differing concepts of the word, Malta was a paradise to none, perhaps, more than the spinster or widow with romance or matrimony in mind. Men heavily outnumbered them, mostly bachelors too, or at least footloose. Girls grew up in Malta under the impression that ships were put there to dance on. In those days a dance or party or function of some kind occupied wardroom or quarter-deck every evening in three ships out of four. Few, except by inclination, avoided being a guest at one of the governor's three palaces, or at Admiralty House in Valletta where the Commander-in-Chief lived, or Admiralty House in Vittoriosa, where the Admiral Superintendent lived. Acquaintanceships born at such affairs blossomed and fructified – or were nipped – on the baked earth of the tennis courts or golf course or polo ground at the Marsa, the great sports arena and officers' club with the racetrack around it, beyond the head of Grand Harbour.

Weekend picnics and moonlight bathing parties were popular in the bays around the island. On the cultural side, there was opera of almost five-star quality at a real opera house. Leading tenors and *prime donne* came over from Naples and Rome and Palermo for the season and the Maltese chorus included some richly uninhibited songstresses. About the only social activity in which British personnel and Maltese upper class condescended to mix with each other was the theatrical ventures of the Malta Amateur Dramatic Club ; although a certain amount of semi-official fraternising went on during the annual carnival and at the traditional *bal masqué* at the opera house. If, in the absence of the fleet, a girl felt lonely, she had only to visit the ' snake pit ', as the ladies' lounge of the Union Club in Valletta was affectionately called, to indulge her inclinations for gentle character-assassination of absent friends – or learn the business from experts.

' Jack ashore ' found Malta of the twenties equally an island of dreams. " Beer twopence-halfpenny a pint," the old sailor muses, " steak, ham and chips, with eggs, a shilling. As fine a bit of coastline as any I knew, for bathing and sailing."

The tinsel glamour of the ' Gut ' – ' Come in, Jack, all your ship's company inside, both dronk.' Every kind of sport except ice hockey ; good clean competitive stuff, and a keenness never surpassed on school playing field or international stadium, in the fleet soccer finals at the Corradino ground. . . .

CHAPTER II

The Fleet Flagship

' *And ships in thousands lay below,*
And men in nations, all were his.'

IT might almost have been said of the Commander-in-Chief
of the British Mediterranean fleet in the spring of 1928 when
he looked over the ' rocky brow ' of the fort on Grand
Harbour. To say that, when the fleet was in, you could not
see the water for ships would be to exaggerate; but the
whole of Grand Harbour, and its triple inlets of Calcara,
Dockyard and French creeks, as well as the bifurcated roadstead of Sliema and Marsamuscetto north of the promontory
over which Valletta sprawled, were so congested with
funnels and superstructures and awnings that, when you
gazed down from the ramparts, it looked no impossible task
for an agile scrambler to cross the water on foot, using the
monolithic grey battleships and the slim grey cruisers and
destroyers as stepping-stones.

In the centre of Grand Harbour, moored bow and stern
at buoys 1 and 1*a*, lay the fleet flagship, H.M.S. *Queen
Elizabeth*. Astern of her in their appointed berths (which
depended on the relative seniority of their commanding
officers) rose the craggy 150-foot towers of six similar
battleships, each getting on for 30,000 tons displacement and
each mounting eight 15-inch guns: the *Warspite, Valiant*

9

and *Barham*; the *Ramillies, Resolution* and *Royal Oak*; located, by long tradition, in the Mediterranean – the British Navy's heavy brigade and its greatest concentration of hitting power. They made up what was known as the First Battle Squadron.

A bird's-eye view of the harbour would have taken in long lines of dots and dashes running past the seven flat ovals of these monsters, and stretching away beyond them into the shallower water at the Marsa end, the original haven of Valletta. The dots were the cruiser buoys and the dashes the cruisers, First and Third Squadrons plus a few independent ones, a total of about twenty ships on an average day when the fleet was in. They were nearly all of the ' C ' and ' D ' classes, of 4,100 and 4,600 tons, armed with 6-inch guns: *Calypso, Cairo, Cardiff, Calcutta* . . . *Delhi, Dauntless, Dragon, Despatch* – shapes known and names familiar to the inhabitants of many Mediterranean seaports, whose picturesque harbours they rendered more picturesque. With their long sloping forecastles, raked funnels and bridges and their longer, lower sterns, the light cruisers assembled at Malta in the twenties were among the most graceful and functional-looking warships ever seen.

The destroyers numbered between thirty-five and forty as a rule. Not a sailor on that station, except the rawest of recent arrivals, but could identify them from the pendants they flew and could rattle off their names as they filed, in one apparently interminable pageant, in or out of the creeks where their moorings were laid: *Vanessa, Viscount, Vanoc, Vanquisher, Vega, Vimiera, Vivacious* . . . the destroyers were still neatly arranged by initial letter, and the building programme, having just finished with the post-war ' V ' and ' W ' classes, was about to start the alphabet again with *Amazon* and *Ambuscade*.

Battleships, cruisers and destroyers were considered the real constituents of a fleet in 1928. There were submarines – about sixteen of them at Malta – but they belonged to a small esoteric world of their own, meeting their more conventional fellow-members only two or three times a year, in exercises. There were aircraft-carriers, two giants, the 22,000-ton *Eagle* and *Courageous* – but lumped together in the despised category of ' other vessels ', their functions not yet altogether appreciated in every quarter. There were also hosts of miscellaneous small and specialist craft – seaplane carriers and depot ships, sloops and mine-sweepers, monitors and minelayers.

Occasional notable visitors to Malta (but more often operating from Gibraltar and not always forming part of the Mediterranean command) were the 27,000-ton battle-cruisers *Renown* and *Repulse*. Sometimes the cruiser squadrons were temporarily augmented with one or two of a heavier class – *Effingham* or *Frobisher* or *Hawkins*; sometimes one of the big new ' County ' class cruisers joined up for a while, bound for the Far East perhaps and getting rid of her teething troubles *en route*.

With sport and recreation ashore comprehensively organised, letters home from the fleet at Malta must often have given an impression of a life of Saturday-afternoon pleasures and sybaritic *far niente*. But this was a period of intense activity for the fleet. Singly or in flotillas and squadrons, sailing for exercises, returning from exercises, shifting berths in the harbour to prepare for exercises, the ships were constantly on the move. No main-line railway terminus saw so much coming and going of steam in the course of a day; no traffic controller at international airport led so hectic an existence as did the King's Harbourmaster and the Staff Officer (Operations) at Malta.

Some days the fleet in company would muster a hundred ships and more, and if it happened to be a royal birthday, or some occasion on which they were dressed overall, Grand Harbour would be a garden of rippling coloured flags. Next day Malta might awake to find all its inlets deserted, all the units hull down on the horizon, represented only by wisps of smoke and the tugs returning. It was at times like this, when the Commander-in-Chief took the fleet to sea for manoeuvres or a cruise, that one realised that Malta also supported a big garrison of soldiers, and a few airmen, and a huge civilian population. Then one saw the shore-based bachelors coming into their own, possibly even a member of the ' fishing fleet ' strolling, unescorted and bored with life, down Kingsway (they called it Strada Reale then) in Valletta.

The ' big ships ' – this meant the capital ships, the 15-inch battleships, most of them fairly up-to-date, none more than twelve years old, only recently superseded by the three United States ' Marylands ', the two Japanese ' Mutsus ' and (greatest of all) Britain's own *Rodney* and *Nelson* as the most powerful objects afloat in the world – the big ships steamed many thousands of miles during a Mediterranean commission that normally lasted nearer three years than two. Gunpower was their *raison d'être* and gunnery occupied most of the time, thought and energy of their complement. High-angle shoots at smoke-bursts or sleeve targets towed by aircraft; main armament and secondary armament full-

calibre and sub-calibre firings at surface targets towed by
tugs and destroyers; throw-off shoots at other big ships . . .
director tests, turret tests, inclination tests, control party
exercises, concentration exercises, test firings and battle-
practice for the annual competition: for one reason and
another, unless undergoing boiler-cleaning or refit in dock,
the big ship was at sea most week-days. Three times a year,
in winter, spring and summer, she left Malta altogether for a
cruise lasting two weeks or more.

The cruisers followed a similar routine. But 'small
ships' – meaning destroyers and little else – though operating from the same base and sharing the same exercise
areas, saw practically nothing of their larger consorts from
week to week. When in harbour, they moored round the
corner from the big ships, in Sliema creek, with perhaps a
light cruiser or two, the overflow from a chock-a-block Grand
Harbour, to keep them company. They went to sea in
flotillas, ranged the Aegean and Adriatic and Ionian seas, were
shuffled and reshuffled in high-speed manoeuvres by senior
officers with the manipulative dexterity of card-sharpers.
They exercised guns too, and torpedoes and minesweeping
gear and seamanship and were lately dabbling in the new
pastime of hunting submarines with asdic. Now and again
they went off in twos and threes to show the flag in Turkey
and Yugoslavia, Spain and Italy and the south of France.

Their officers and ship's companies rarely mixed with
those of the battleships and cruisers when ashore. They
were supposed to have bred a keener but less formal *esprit*
in their cramped quarters than the sailors of the roomier,
steadier, more barracks-like big ships, whom they held in
friendly contempt. The Mediterranean fleet destroyer

captains, in particular, were proverbial among naval officers the world over at that epoch for their *panache*, ebullience, irreverence and eccentricities. Usually they got away with it: they rarely met their Commander-in-Chief, rarely saw a battleship, except to fire torpedoes at her during a fleet exercise twice a year.

The naval Commander-in-Chief at Malta in 1928 was the British armed forces' outstanding living personality, beside whom contemporary generals and admirals appeared as nonentities : Admiral Sir Roger Keyes. Short of stature and brisk of temper, wiry, vigorous, nimble as a cabin boy and alive with ambition, he was coming to the end of his term in the finest active command the Royal Navy had to offer, was still a mere stripling, as admirals go, of fifty-four – and was the obvious choice for First Sea Lord when that post next fell vacant.

Keyes's biographer, Brigadier Aspinall-Oglander, told of a man ' who had become a legend even while he was still alive . . . a passionate exponent of the value of the offensive in war . . . he expunged the word impossible from his dictionary and difficulties were to him a challenge and even an invitation.

' In China in 1900, while still a young lieutenant, he captured with thirty bluejackets a fort which Russian and German generals, with four thousand men at their disposal, had deemed too dangerous to attack. . . . In the first World War the organiser and hero of the immortal raid on Zeebrugge, he was largely responsible at a critical hour for saving this country from the desperate menace of the U-boats. . . . So high was his reputation for courage and resource that I am assured by one of his shipmates, himself a V.C., that numberless young officers who had never seen him, when faced with a difficult problem in the last war, would ask themselves: " I wonder what Keyes would have done ? " '

A dramatic rise such as his, over the heads of brilliant officers, is not made without making enemies too. All his life Keyes had critics: ' Too prone to thrust himself forward ', was how old Admiral Seymour viewed the China business. ' Thinks more of his own advancement than of the good of the Service ', was the verdict of another Commander-in-Chief. Accounts of his part in the Dardanelles operations, as chief of staff to the naval commander, sent cold shudders through some thoughtful tacticians. He had obstinately lobbied for a death-or-glory assault with Britain's latest battleship that would have very likely ensured, whichever ship he was to hoist his flag in when he became a Commander-in-Chief himself, it would not be the *Queen Elizabeth*, for she would have been sacrificed. Keyes maintained to the end of his days, contemptuously dismissing all argument about it, that the Dardanelles withdrawal was ' one of the most dastardly and cowardly surrenders in the history of our country '.

His warmest admirers recognised faults in him: pigheadedness, disinclination to admit an error, a tendency (which was equally a virtue) to adopt a plan and stick to it. He was a leader for whom the intellectual *clique*, however, had no time: ' a fighting blockhead ', Admiral Richmond called him, ' – courageous, independent, but with very little brain '.

Zeebrugge, on St George's Day, 1918, brought Keyes an

early knighthood, ten thousand pounds and the idolatry of a nation. In the list of household names that emerged from that war, his ran a close third to those of Jellicoe and Beatty. His climb to the highest peaks of the promotion mountain was rapid and smooth, and he roped two boyhood friends behind him for the ascent. They were Dudley Pound and Wilfred Tomkinson.

One reason, it was believed, why Lord Beatty kept the post of First Sea Lord for seven long years after Versailles was that he was waiting until Sir Roger was ready to step into his shoes; he had been Keyes's champion and protector for a long time. But Lord Beatty's resignation, coming suddenly in 1927, put the younger admiral in a quandary. He eventually decided to stay on at Malta for the final year of his term of office. He regarded the First Sea Lord then installed – Sir Charles Madden – as a kind of *locum*.

A Commander-in-Chief's reluctance to give up the Mediterranean, even to be head of the Navy, was understandable; especially in Sir Roger Keyes's case. He had greatly enriched, if not created, the social and sporting scene at Malta, and was in his element showing off his magnificent fleet to friends and politicians, foreign potentates and aristocratic and influential birds of passage. The Governor used to complain that Sir Roger did all his entertaining for him – Admiralty House, not Verdala Palace or San Antonio, was the principal guest-house for V.I.P.s on the island. One memorable fortnight it was young Randolph Churchill with his uncle Jack, whom Winston later described as having had ' the holiday of his life '. Another time the Duke of York, later King George VI, stopped off from an empire tour in H.M.S. *Renown* to play polo for the Commander-in-Chief's team at the Marsa. The First Lord of the Admiralty (W. C. Bridgeman) and the First Sea Lord (Beatty) had been frequent and appreciative visitors. 'Come on with me to Malta', wrote Keyes at the time of the latter's resignation. 'Play polo, attend a race-meeting and when you leave you will get a send-off (from the fleet) such as no one ever had in naval history'.

Polo had been Admiral Keyes's liveliest passion from the time he joined the Service. He kept his own string of ponies and raced them as well. Years earlier, in China, he had disobeyed an order to sail because of a prior engagement at the polo ground. More recently, professional rivalry had been discrediting him at home with gossip that he was turning the ratings' football pitches at the Corradino over to polo.

Lord Louis Mountbatten captained Keyes's polo team, the 'Centurions' – the naval polo succession runs through a dynasty of distinguished personages, from Prince Louis of Battenberg, Beatty, Keyes and Lord Louis to the Duke of Edinburgh in the nineteen-sixties. Lady Keyes and her three daughters made up another team, the 'Bunch of Keyes', and ladies and guests of the household a third, called 'Admiralty House'. The Admiralty House four were out most mornings before breakfast at the Marsa, playing against teams of midshipmen and novices. Late at night the admiral conducted tactical exercises with model ponies on the big billiard table, where his predecessors had manoeuvred model warships. And all day long the game was going on somewhere in the island, with pony-flesh and racing the main topic of conversation in certain clubs and wardrooms and a great number of officers – a few genuine enthusiasts, a lot with an opportunist eye to favour, who had scarcely heard of *chukkas* until they got to Malta – in the thick of it. In Portsmouth or Pall Mall, Bermuda or Hong Kong, when someone spoke of a polo promotion, every sailor and everyone who had recently been to Malta knew what he meant.

One young officer arrived to join the fleet flagship on the Mediterranean station carrying, with disarming impudence, a polo stick under one arm and a copy of *Debrett* under the other: symbols of two sure passports, he implied, to fortune. A roll-call of the officers in H.M.S. *Queen Elizabeth* in 1928 would have sounded a little like a courtly assembly of the olden time. More than a polo team might have been raised among the peers on Sir Roger's staff. Even the midshipmen undergoing training in the flagship – only a dozen, but hand-picked like the rest of his officers – included two lords, a baronet and an earl's son. There were so many double- and treble-barrelled names in the wardroom into the bargain that when one of the officers picked up a dog on the Greek islands and made a mascot of it, the ship's company christened it Barker-Barker.

Two great-grandchildren of Queen Victoria served in the First Battle Squadron. One was squadron gunnery officer, Commander the Marquess of Milford Haven; the other his younger brother, Lieutenant Lord Louis Mountbatten (later Earl Mountbatten of Burma), who had just come out to assist Lieutenant-Commander Sir Philip Bowyer-Smith, the fleet wireless telegraphy officer. W/T officers were a new and rare addition to the Navy's specialists. Most fleets had none yet, or only one; Keyes had acquired two. They seemed to be a cult rather than a branch, so far – addicted to satin ties and breast-pocket handkerchiefs and Tattersall waistcoats.

Lord Louis, for all his social disadvantages, became an exceptional W/T officer. A telegraphist who served under him recalls how the operating procedure on the fleet communication waves, which was chaotic when he arrived, had been 'pretty good' by the time he left. An old chief telegraphist remembers him as 'one of the few officers I ever met who could actually send and read Morse code properly'.

'Are you coming out to see the Fleet,' wrote Admiral Keyes to Mr Winston Churchill, the Chancellor of the Exchequer, '*while we still have one*?'

By 1928 it was clear that the Government was damming the stream of naval expenditure to a trickle, that when the St George's cross of the Admiral's personal flag came down from the maintop of the *Queen Elizabeth* it would mark the surrender of the Mediterranean fleet's ancient glory. More enlightened and more intelligent admirals were to follow Keyes to Malta; but he was the last of the line of great autocratic, flamboyant personalities who had been laying down the law and balancing power from this pivot of an island since Napoleonic days.

One manifestation of Keyes's greatness, or at least of his talent for doing things in a big way, was the huge and elaborate staff organisation he created at Malta. It was not only in the wireless telegraphy world that he wanted two of everything. The *Queen Elizabeth*, one of the biggest battleships ever seen in Grand Harbour, was hard put to it to accommodate the extra burden of staff officers (mostly of fairly important rank, demanding cabins appropriate to

their status) he imposed on her. Keyes's old friends headed
the list: Rear-Admiral Dudley Pound, his chief of staff,
went home in 1927 to be assistant chief of the naval staff in
Whitehall and pave the way for Sir Roger's arrival; and
was relieved by Rear-Admiral Wilfred Tomkinson.

From the flagship, or its headquarters ashore, the staff
poured bright ideas over the fleet on behalf of the Commander-in-Chief. But every squadron and flotilla had its
own junior admiral as well, with a staff of his own, doing the
same thing on a more modest scale. Battleships were the
responsibility of Vice-Admiral John Donald Kelly, who
bore the title of Vice-Admiral commanding First Battle
Squadron and also deputised for the Commander-in-Chief
in his absence.

Admiral Kelly, known everywhere as Joe, had the useful
reputation of being a character – one of those bluff and
breezy seadogs whom anecdotes stick to like burrs, who are
credited with a whole phrase-book of *bons mots* and who go
through life wrapped in a cosy armour of legend. Joe's
popularity derived partly from his alleged loathing for a
brother, Howard, another vice-admiral (currently in
China); the feeling was said to be mutual and their periodical insults to each other by signal passed quickly into naval
lore.

When Joe Kelly addressed ship's companies from a
capstan on the quarter-deck, he was garrulous, unaffected and
worth listening to. For civilians he had no conversation
whatever, and he made an embarrassing hash of speeches at
functions ashore. Keyes was the same: a toastmaster's gavel
and a row of stiff shirt-fronts frightened the hero of Zeebrugge to death. But these were days when verbal constipa-

tion in a naval officer was counted a virtue. " I haven't the gift of the gab, my lads," was about the most endearing sentiment any captain or admiral could express: it was supposed to prove his innate honesty, his antipathy to the disreputable occupations of sea-lawyer and politician. Reporting on one occasion of state when he saw Roger Keyes, as usual, fail to string three coherent words together, another famous admiral wrote quite sincerely: " He could hardly speak today. I liked him for that."

Both Keyes and his second-in-command were lucky in having subordinates for whom ' speechifying ', as they liked to call it then, was no ordeal. The Commander-in-Chief's was his flag-captain, T. S. V. Phillips – later Admiral ' Tom ' Phillips, who was lost in the *Repulse-Prince of Wales* catastrophe in 1941. The Vice-Admiral's was *his* flag-captain, J. F. Somerville, a heroic figure of the second World War and eventually an Admiral of the Fleet.

Kelly ran the First Battle Squadron from H.M.S. *Warspite*. The six battleships were organised in two divisions and there was another admiral to handle the junior division. This was always a rear-admiral's job, one of the humblest of flag-officers' appointments, to which a newly promoted one was nearly always sent. He didn't stay more than a year, as a rule. In 1927 and 1928, except for short interruptions, the second flagship in the First Battle Squadron at Malta was H.M.S. *Royal Oak*; and in that period Rear-Admirals Norris, Collard and Kerr flew their flags in her.

Not only laymen found the command pyramid a little confusing and top-heavy looking. An older generation of officers thought so too – those who remembered times when one admiral had done practically everything himself with twice as many ships, getting along somehow with scarcely any staff at all. It was not confusing, but it was frustrating, to younger captains, perhaps their own masters in earlier appointments who, expecting to demonstrate their fitness for high command, were shown, as soon as they came to the Mediterranean fleet, that their routine was so comprehensively organised they were left with nothing to do ' except ', as one put it, ' to say what time you wanted a call in the morning and whether you would have a cup of tea '.

New arrivals to Keyes's command sensed, amid the chatter and gaiety ashore and the never-a-dull-moment programme on board, overtones of strain and short temper. The Navy's working day was expected to run with clock-work precision and no one would argue with that; but now pleasures were strictly timed and recreation regimented. The aim seemed to be to record the activity of every man on board for twenty-four hours in the day, to make sure not a minute was wasted or left unaccounted for. Daily, weekly, monthly and annual reports scheduled and standardised all leisure pursuits. Ships had to send details of football teams and spectators landed daily; when the officers went shooting, even the size and description of the bag was required by the flagship. ' Everything was counted, from the game slaughtered on the hunt to the sling-stones deposited in the official arsenals.' Louis Baudin wrote that of the Inca bureaucracy, but it applied precisely to the Mediterranean command in the Keyes era.

Suspicions that their commands were no longer their own became certainties when captains pored over the orders for a big fleet exercise – or, better still, for the annual exercises of the combined fleets, Atlantic and Mediterranean. They went into volumes of closely printed instructions, a detailed time-table of events for all, laid down by the all-powerful staff with Teutonic thoroughness and an oriental disregard for domestic convenience or private inclination.

The precision was alarming: the orders would state at exactly what hour, in what direction, what order and what distance apart, ships would enter harbour twenty days ahead; a schedule of the how, when and where of sporting fixtures on arrival (everything but a forecast of the results, in fact); the squadron dispositions and alterations for every moment of the passage from one place to another (regardless of possible interference by, for instance, stray merchant shipping); instructions to cover any tiny gap left in the programme, as ' Noon: Hands will be piped to bathe ' (ignoring the possibility that the weather might not be suitable by then, or the water full of jellyfish) – all this and much more might be found in the Mediterranean fleet's orders for a series of exercises. They were monumental works – or would have been – monuments to the administrative stamina and efficiency of the staff, had they not been also susceptible to instant dissolution by some unforeseen contingency. At the beginning of such a set of orders, it needed only a delay in sailing to put the whole machine out of gear and render months of planning useless.

This is what happened in the middle of March 1928. Something went wrong. The unprecedented occurred, the fleet failed to leave harbour at the appointed time for its rendezvous with the Atlantic squadrons off Alboran island – and spectators on the ramparts of Valletta could not have been more shaken if they had seen the battleships and cruisers and destroyers suddenly subside beneath the surface of Grand Harbour and Sliema creek.

Hours late, all the warships began to get under way: first, the fleet flagship, H.M.S. *Queen Elizabeth*, with several long hoists flying from her halyards and above them the flag of the Commander-in-Chief; then H.M.S. *Warspite*, wearing the flag of Vice-Admiral John Kelly; then the rest of the Battle Squadron, then the cruiser flagships and their squadrons, then a single aircraft-carrier. Out from the Marsamuscetto entrance proceeded the destroyer leaders and their flotillas, darting off in all directions to form the screens their exercise diagrams prescribed. The cruisers went ahead. The fleet settled down to its dispositions and all along the lines the Morse and semaphore signals went, repairing the wreck of the programme, cancelling serial orders by the dozen and distributing amendments by the score.

Malta was empty of ships. A new arrival on the island, looking over the creeks and the roadsteads in the spring sunshine on Thursday, the 15th of March, would have seen, in the almost complete absence of white ensigns afloat, justification of a claim being made that afternoon in the House of Commons in London: ' This country has done more in the direction of disarmament and scrapping ships than any other nation since the armistice '.

The words were spoken by Mr W. C. Bridgeman, First Lord of the Admiralty in Stanley Baldwin's Conservative government, when he presented the Navy estimates for the forthcoming year – pre-general-election year. They totalled a little more than fifty-seven million pounds – the little more being earmarked for the air arm of the fleet, to provide ' a new type of aircraft '. It was a lower figure than those the experts had been forecasting. In spite of substantial increases in costs since the war, it was about the same as the estimates for 1914; and about as much as would build one new aircraft-carrier in the estimates of 1965.

In his survey of the Navy's year, Mr Bridgeman mentioned other satisfactory statistics. He gave details of the numbers of naval officers who were passing through the new Imperial Defence College, which had a sailor – Vice-Admiral Sir Herbert Richmond – for its president. They had all learned something there, said the First Lord, from their contacts with the officers of the other two Services. He referred to the scheme for taking boy seamen out of the gloomy, insanitary hulks afloat at Portsmouth, about which he had 'never been very happy', and re-establishing them ashore in a new school to be called H.M.S. *St Vincent*. And, in support of a statement that the morale of the fleet had never been higher, he reported that the annual number of courts martial in recent years had gone down dramatically and in 1927 reached its lowest figure ever – fourteen, one-tenth of the figure for 1912. ' Offences against superior authority ' in the same period had dropped from one hundred and two to four.

It was in that passage in his speech which dealt with the Washington naval conference that the First Lord revealed the stimulating lead Britain had given to disarmament. When the 1914-18 war ended, the nation had had 1,538 ships; now she had 405. During the year under review, links with the Kaiser's war had been snapping among personnel also: announcing Lord Beatty's resignation ' at last ',

Mr Bridgeman reminded the House, in a noticeably re-strained eulogy, that not least among the First Sea Lord's qualities had been a talent for speaking his mind. "He was an extremely good debater and well able to hold his own with the present Chancellor of the Exchequer" – a good-natured grin at this from Winston Churchill.

Moving the Labour Party's amendment, Mr L. McNeill Weir, the 'shadow' First Lord, told the Government that now was the time for a great gesture in the cause of peace. For a start, he urged, Britain should make a clean sweep of every battleship and submarine she had, build no more cruisers and abolish all existing ones above a certain tonnage.

The debate continued throughout the evening, a Con-servative member, Mr A. Williams, raising the expected laugh by advising the First Lord to concentrate on reducing the shore establishments before he touched the ships, for he had a feeling that "when the dreams of the honourable gentlemen opposite are almost realised and the Navy is reduced to one man, he will be found at the Admiralty".

It was almost midnight when the last of a series of votes for expenditure was agreed to. The chamber had been emptying and scarcely forty M.P.s remained in their places to hear the Conservative member for Maidstone say the last and, it appeared, least relevant word on the Navy estimates for that day, just as the House was about to rise.

"I understand that a statement is going to be issued to the press," said Commander Carlyon Bellairs, "to the effect that the Captain and some of the officers of the *Royal Oak* have refused to sail under Admiral Collard, have been court-martialled, and have been carried as passengers to Gibraltar. . . .

" I suggest the Admiralty issue as soon as possible the actual state of the case."

The First Lord had gone home and it was left to Lieu-tenant-Colonel Headlam, Parliamentary Secretary to the Admiralty, to reply that he could not, at that moment, give any answer or make any comment.

CHAPTER III

The Midshipman's Log

On a dirty evening in January 1926 the midshipman joined
his first seagoing ship. The trot-boat that brought him and
his sea-chest down from Chatham bumped against a thickly
fendered gangway in the swirling ebb of the Medway.
Spears of sleet whipped across the marshes and sparkled in
the swaying searchlight beams of a pair of yardarm groups.
He climbed a long, long ladder, feeling like Jack going up
the beanstalk and wondering what giants awaited him at the
top. On the quarter-deck, in the light fitfully shed by a
wavering backbone illumination circuit, he saluted the
officer of the watch.

"Come aboard to join, sir."

The deck looked as though white paint had been poured
over it and left to set. Next morning he would recognise
this for bare wood, sanded and scrubbed and holystoned to
that purity of colour, like the quarter-decks of all the battleships in the squadron. The brightwork threw a golden
gleam across his path as he stumbled forward towards the
gunroom, following a bo'sun's mate: the polished plate at
the gangway head, the burnished bollards and stanchions
and the brass handrails round the captain's hatch, the crested
tompions in the two great gun-muzzles, the name-plate
ROYAL OAK in big golden bas-relief lettering on the after
screen. By night they caught a reflection from the upper

28

deck lighting, by day – even a sunless winter day at Sheerness – they would dazzle, and the high-gloss paintwork of
the turrets and barbettes and gun barrels would mirror the
flash.

Someone showed him where to sling his hammock and
the gunroom sub-lieutenant gave him the rest of the evening
to settle in – which meant unpacking and writing a note
home and mugging up the gunroom standing orders. In
two days' time, when he was supposed to have found his
way about the ship (although, tramping and climbing
through seven decks, each a thousand feet long and chopped
into hundreds of compartments, he wondered whether he
would ever learn to travel about in her without getting lost),
he would join the other midshipmen, ten of them, at their
instruction and take his share of the duties traditionally
reserved for them – running errands, mostly, for captain or
commander or officer of the watch for the first six months;
and then, perhaps, command of a boat, one of those picturesque little brass-funnelled picket-boats that one could
almost believe to be one's own private warship.

But long before then – within a few days of his arrival, in
fact – the *Royal Oak* would have 'weighed and proceeded',
as the official phrase had it, not to see Sheerness or the
Medway or even the shores of England again for a while.
With four sister battleships she was leaving home waters
for a commission in foreign parts.

Mishaps at sea were commoner in 1926 than they are
today, and the *Royal Oak* was scarcely out of sight of the
Lizard before the hymn, 'Eternal Father, strong to save',
which they sang sometimes at divisions on the quarter-deck
(the thousand-strong ship's company with caps off and hair

blowing in the breeze, the chaplain's white surplice fluttering) began to have real significance. Like most boys, the
midshipman had an eye for the macabre and the opening of
the journal he was taught to keep is a page of death and
disaster:

' At half-past nine the Fleet weighed and proceeded for
Gibraltar. We were in company with *Revenge* and *Ramillies*
The first night at sea the *Wolfhound*, one of our destroyer
screen, ran down a sailing-vessel but saved the crew. She
lost her own first lieutenant. . . . On the morning of the
14th January the *Resolution, Royal Sovereign* and *Furious*
joined the flag. The *Furious* flew off some of her planes, but
the weather was unsuitable and one of them crashed, the
crew being picked up by a destroyer.'

Twenty-four hours later, at anchor in Vigo bay, he saw
the Spaniards abandon their sardine-fishing at the approach
of the fleet and take instead to the more lucrative task of
trawling for refuse down-tide from the battleships.

' In the evening, when libertymen were waiting to come
off, Leading Seaman Lynch fell off the pier, stunning himself, and was drowned. He was buried ashore the next
day.'

On arrival at Gibraltar:

' Marine Watson was found dead this morning. A hatch
had dropped on his chest and suffocation followed.'

' A.B. Adam fell from a window ashore last night . . .
his funeral is tomorrow.'

Three deaths in one ship in the first week of the commission: it was an ominous start.

But, after the funerals, the games. Wherever two or
three of H.M. ships were gathered, sporting fixtures and

competitive seamanship and gunnery exercises took place as a matter of course. For a newly commissioned ship's company, the ' Oaks ' did well at Gibraltar in the football matches and sailing races and battle-firings. Despite those three disturbing tragedies, Captain Seymour must have felt reasonably contented with his ship and her crew, already up among the leaders at work and play. A reputation for hospitality – more important than one might think, on a highly entertainment-conscious station – had early been remarked upon. The midshipman wrote:

' 20th February 1926. At Gibraltar. In the evening the *Royal Oak* was " at home " to the officers of the fleet. The Commander-in-Chief said it was the best-organised entertainment he had ever been to on board a ship ! '

Next month the midshipman got his picket-boat and one of his first jobs was to take an impressive collection of silver sailing and athletics trophies over to the *Revenge* for safe keeping. The *Royal Oak* was leaving the Atlantic fleet here. In a few days, as she steamed eastward, she would sight an approaching clump of smoke-smudges, which would reveal themselves in half an hour as the fighting tops of the battle-ships of the Third Squadron, led by H.M.S. *Iron Duke*, homeward bound from Malta. The *Royal Oak*, going there to fill one of the vacancies they left, would clear lower deck and cheer them as they passed.

' 22nd March 1926. Entered the Grand Harbour, Malta, about nine o'clock and berthed between Number 3 and 3a buoys.'

For a time the new arrivals had the anchorage to themselves, for all the ships were out on manoeuvres. Then:

' . . . The Mediterranean fleet arrived in the afternoon.

Ceres, Coventry and the destroyers went into Sliema, the rest came into Grand Harbour. The Commander-in-Chief, Admiral Sir Roger Keyes, came on board after divisions. The officers were presented and the ship's company marched past.'

At Malta the social, sporting and gunnery round intensified. The life left even the midshipmen exhausted. Eyes, hands, legs and brains were required to be continually in action, or at instant readiness. One must never be caught doing nothing, on duty or off—that was the deadliest sin. The midshipman's log records only extra-curricular activities. On top of these, he was working a normal day, attending instruction and sometimes keeping a watch at night.

Sunday (begins a typical week): a parade through the streets of Valletta, for which H.M.S. *Royal Oak* had to train a contingent in a hurry. Divisions and church and then Harry Goulding the chaplain took all the midshipmen away in the launch for a picnic. The boat broke down and they were not home until midnight.

Monday: a quiet day, because they were all sitting examinations. In the evening a cricket match against the wardroom (Officers 63 and 76, Midshipmen 213 for 4).

Tuesday: The *Royal Oak* went early to sea, to the exercise area, for 6-inch and 15-inch practice firing. Returning to harbour, she met the *Warspite*, coming out to relieve the *Queen Elizabeth* while the latter went to England for modernisation. All eyes were on this reconditioned monster's changed shape, her anti-torpedo bulges, and the two funnels now merged into one. In harbour, in the afternoon, the midshipmen took platoons in rifle drill and in the evening,

REAR-ADMIRAL B. ST G. COLLARD, C.B., D.S.O.

after they had attended the captain's wife at a tea party, the ship sailed again for a sub-calibre night shoot.

Wednesday: Having returned to harbour at dawn, the *Royal Oak* sent competitors to the range at Ricasoli for the fleet rifle meeting. The midshipmen came back early, because they were detailed for an athletics meeting with the cruiser *Ceres*. In the evening they pulled cutters in a challenge race against another cruiser. That night the ship slipped from the buoy and went to sea again, for a full-calibre shoot with the main armament. It was the first time many had experienced 15-inch broadside firing. 'Made the ship rock considerably,' the midshipman noted. 'The shooting was bad.'

It is all bad, or slow, in the *Royal Oak* at this stage of the commission, as it is with every new ship on the station. It takes time to work up to the standards old habitués of the fleet have painfully attained, under Sir Roger and his relentless staff. The midshipman's journal continues with the dreary tale of a great occasion, the squadron sports meeting at the Marsa:

Thursday: ' Our heavy tug-o'-war team was well beaten by the *Queen Elizabeth's* . . . owing to a misunderstanding our light team was not allowed to pull . . . the obstacle team scratched . . . our representatives did not win anything.'

The ' Oaks ' had been wearing themselves out, early in the morning, during the dinner hour and late at night, practising for nothing.

Individual ship loyalty produced wild excitement at events like these, as at the annual regatta. It kept the betting heavy too (professional bookmakers were installed in the bigger ships in those days, and the odds signalled round the fleet and transmitted to units on distant parts of the station) – but the favourite usually carried the day and the favourite was always the ship that had been at Malta longest. On this occasion H.M.S. *Barham* was the veteran of the First Battle Squadron and she won the cup from the *Malaya*, who was going home to recommission.

Friday: From seven a.m. the midshipman checked ammunition into and out of a lighter at the periodical exchange of over-age shells. He rushed away from that to join the racing gig's crew at practice. The ship sent the seamen away for a squadron sailing-race in whalers outside the breakwater and, for once, *Royal Oak* came second out of five starters. That evening she herself went outside for turret tests, and her boats ran shuttle services to Customs House steps and Parlatorio wharf, ferrying off the many working parties and sports teams, in weather that fast deteriorated until the small craft had to be hoisted. The diarist clattered down to the gunroom wet but elated at having brought the picket-boat back full of men and got it hooked on to the derrick and inboard without a hitch; telling his fellow midshipmen it was so rough off St Elmo's point he was not sure whether he had come round the breakwater or over it.

Saturday: The ship 'weighed and proceeded' at six o'clock, following the *Barham* and the *Resolution* out of harbour, for a full-scale fleet exercise, a foretaste of the month-long manoeuvres shortly to come. The Commander-in-Chief in his temporary flagship, the *Warspite*, was already at sea with an aircraft-carrier and both the cruiser squadrons. An inclination exercise, a throw-off shoot, a night encounter, a test for lookouts, a searchlight visibility experiment, a sub-calibre anti-aircraft shoot, equal speed manoeuvres with commanders acting as captains and first lieutenants as navigators, a ' darken ship ' evolution – and they all steamed home in the early hours of Sunday, in time for divisions and church on their respective quarter-decks and later in the forenoon a sailing race for the Commander-in-Chief's cup. There were such mounds of trophies distributed about the Mediterranean fleet that one could be certain of something coming forward, at least once a week, to be boxed for, shot for, sailed for or run for. The afternoon was devoted to getting the journals up to date, and compulsory letter writing. The rest of the day was the midshipmen's own – except for the hours during which they had watches to keep.

And so to Monday morning again, and the start of another week of organised bustle, scramble and drudgery. Napoleon's motto, ' *Activité, activité, vitesse* ', might have been composed for the Mediterranean fleet – or perhaps the Red Queen's, ' Faster, faster ! '

To be a part of that whirring, indefatigable machine was an inspiring thing – if you could stand the pace, and when all ran smoothly. But if the apparatus developed a small fault, the whole mechanism shook and ground and squealed. Then, one ' stood from under '. Then, a minor misdemeanour assumed the appearance of a catastrophic offence.

During the first summer cruise of the *Royal Oak's* Mediterranean commission the fleet went to Venice (' Played the town at football and lost three-nil ', says the midshipman's log), to Trieste and down the Dalmatian coast. The word cruise, to the sailor, evokes no picture of deckchairs and swimming pools and sun-tan oil. On fleet cruises, especially Mediterranean fleet cruises, the sea training moved out of top gear and into overdrive. The midshipman filled a page of his journal with notes on the tricky night-passage down the isle-strewn, unlit coast between Trieste and Gravosa (Grusz) – itself a preoccupying exercise, one would have thought, for a squadron of battleships.

'Rejoined flag at seven-thirty p.m. A sub-calibre shoot was carried out, the 15-inch throwing-off at *Warspite* and the 6-inch at *Vampire*. . . . For exercise, ran a line of soundings, getting a cast every three minutes. . . . Battenberg exercises and simple manoeuvres for the officers of the watch. . . . The morning evolution was towing, *Resolution* took *Warspite* in tow and we took a destroyer in tow on each quarter. . . . Before dawn we did a searchlight sweep on the destroyers.'

After everyone had been up for at least a part of the night, the sensational improvement in the ship's sporting record that the Battle Squadron vice-admiral was demanding could hardly be expected at once. It was in any case only those who had not been to Yugoslavia before who were surprised to find themselves up against, not a disorderly, demoralised crowd of under-nourished nondescripts, but squads of lean, lithe, muscular, brown-bodied olympians:

'23rd July 1926. At Gravosa. A water-polo match against Gravosa was lost by ten goals. We also lost two soccer matches. A Service cutter pulling race was held between the battleships and a Yugoslav squadron of four small gunboats over a two-mile course. They entered three crews, who had to pull in our boats, as they had no boats of their own. They got the first three places, *Warspite* was a good fourth and *Royal Oak* easily last.'

Does the British Mediterranean fleet still roam freely among the wild green islands and beautiful sub-tropical harbours of the Adriatic and Aegean seas, enlisting sporting opposition from a polite and co-operative populace ? Do its officers still land for half a day's wildfowling on the iron-curtain seaboard, without passport or visa or permit of any kind? Or its hundreds of armed sailors and marines swarm ashore and capture some old Venetian *kastel* in a landing party exercise? It is doubtful – doubtful whether the fleet's midshipmen will ever write again, as the *Royal Oak's* midshipmen could write, of anchoring between Brioni and the mainland and trying out its ' succulent oranges, v. good polo ground but poor golf course'; or of taking possession of a Greek or Albanian bay for a day or two, to practise for the regatta; or, without a by-your-leave to the locals, running a cross-country race through the streets of a small port in Montenegro.

Kotor in Yugoslavia, Dragamesti bay and Argostoli round the corner in Greece, Pollenza in the Balearics and Marmorice in Turkey: these are names no sailor of the years between the wars can recall without nostalgic memories of the fleet in whites, the ensigns hanging limp against their staves and the staccato bark of the racing cutter's coxswain at early regatta practice, coming across the satin-smooth water in the still morning air. Here the tough-looking battleships would lie, burnished metal and enam-elled paintwork gleaming, and snowy white awnings spread. Lakeside villagers knew them well – the names of

Beatty, Keyes and Kelly were more familiar to them than those of their own kings and presidents.

In the nineteen-sixties, the British fleet probably lies off-shore and meekly requests permission to enter the pretty little harbours of the Adriatic her bluejackets once made free with. The highlands one climbed for the pleasure of look-ing down on a blue bay glittering with white ensigns one may not now even photograph. Coastal protection vessels ensure that no foreign warship gets within much less than radar range of certain coastlines. The recreation isles of the Dalmatian coast are mostly out of bounds.

Some of the big bays will be available still, though crammed with the ghosts of the big ships. It is not likely they are familiar to the naval voyager of today, for all that. The Commander-in-Chief of 1965, with his handful of frigates, has little need of the great lonely, land-locked havens, deeply sheltered, to which his predecessors brought their squadrons in divisions. Only an elderly goat-herd or fisherman, perhaps, misses the sight of them all mooring in formation, with one simultaneous plunge of fifty anchors and one resonant fifty-fold roar of running-out cable.

But in the twenties the Mediterranean sea, from Haifa to Tangier, was *mare nostrum* to the British fleet, before Musso-lini publicised the phrase. Sir Roger accepted no inter-ference from others, not even the Admiralty, although he would go out of his way sometimes to consult his old chief. 'Earl Beatty's yacht *Sheila* is anchored close inshore,' notes the midshipman at Gavrion bay on the isle of Andros. 'It is not clear why we are here.' When, on his own initiative, the Commander-in-Chief sent the *Resolution* to Alexandria to pacify the populace at the request of a nervous old friend he was letting it be known that one man gave the orders for these waters. It was not so much *mare nostrum* as *mare meum*, in Keyes's time.

In August the *Royal Oak* got a new commanding officer, Captain Seymour being promoted to rear-admiral and retiring at his own request. The midshipman's journal recorded the change-over:

' 21st August 1926. At Malta. Captain the Hon. A. C. Strutt took over command of the ship from Captain Seymour. England won the fifth Test match.'

But the *Royal Oak* had won nothing yet and further disappointment attended her when she went off to Volo in Greece for the chief recreational event of the year – the fleet regatta – during the second summer cruise.

' The *Barham* had an extraordinarily good cutter, which won all her races easily. Our first cutter did quite well when it had a decent crew, but the second never managed to be anywhere but last. The skiff lost all its races. The gunroom gig was third in its race. We expected to do much better. The final placings in the Battle Squadron were: *Barham* 280½ points, *Valiant* 231, *Resolution* 180, *Warspite* 136½, *Royal Oak* 96.'

They were all back in Malta by November (the diarist doing well on the bone-hard yellow earth of the Marsa as scrum-half for the ship's rugby team), when the *Royal Oak* became a flagship. Rear-Admiral Norris came out from England to be the junior flag-officer in the First Battle Squadron. He relieved Rear-Admiral Staveley, who had flown his flag in the *Resolution* and was going home in an atmosphere of vague depression. He had quarrelled, rumour said, with his flag-captain, Martyn.

Except that they seemed to be hearing the 'Guard and band' call for the marines much more often, and were summoned to breakfast in the admiral's cabin, in turn, during the first fortnight of the flag-officer's stay, Rear-Admiral Norris's arrival meant as little to the midshipmen as the new captain's had done. But the two changes spelled, or at least coincided with, a turning point in the ship's sporting fortunes, the start of a slow climb that took the *Royal Oak* over the next twelve months to an enviable position in the squadron league tables and list of trophy-holders. The *Resolution's* departure for Devonport removed some of the opposition: she steamed out of Grand Harbour, flying her paying-off pendant and cheered by the companies of assembled ships and knots of spectators far out on the head-lands and tip of St Elmo's point. The *Royal Oak* celebrated early next morning with a notable hockey win over the *Valiant* and, a couple of days later, a crushing one over the *Malaya*.

Caesar cup, Eastbourne cup, Hamilton cup, Beresford cup, Trieste cup – one by one the winter knock-out tourna-ments came and went. The ship spent Christmas in the floating dock, having a short refit, and the midshipmen at least came out new men: they won the inter-ship cross-country race and Admiral Norris showed his appreciation by sending a crate of champagne down to the gunroom.

The diary is blank for a few weeks. The diarist has been overdoing it and is in hospital with jaundice. Most young-sters in the Mediterranean fleet have their off-spells, in 1927. The Battle Squadron's health, in general, is not too good. The midshipman misses a cruise to Greece – more like a holiday, for once, than most; the sailor's idea of a holiday, that is, when it storms and blows so furiously that whole batches of exercises have to be cancelled. The weather keeps the fleet at sea – it would never be fit for pulling or sailing in the most sheltered anchorage this month – and as the capital ships steam slowly into the wind, south of the Strait of Otranto, and a backwash of sea rolls through the case-mates and down on to the messdecks, a destroyer man, catching a glimpse from his own wildly tossing craft across a valley of water and blown spray, suggests with all the disdain of the small-ship sailor for big-ship life that ' they've very likely had to postpone the petty officers' billiards tourna-ment in the battlewagons today '.

' 9th February 1927. *Royal Oak* 659, *Warspite* 638, *Malaya* 638, *Valiant* 389 ' – only the seasonal torpedo-loading drill results, but it deserved a red-ink entry in the midshipman's log. At last the ' Oaks ' were top in some-thing. The new captain had done the trick (the ship was ' private ' once more, Rear-Admiral Norris having shifted his flag temporarily to the recently returned *Royal Sovereign*); or she had been long enough on the station to be ' Keyed up ' in proper Mediterranean fashion. It was no flash in the pan. Sunday after Sunday, the journal reports, from this time onwards, one admiral or another was received aboard the *Royal Oak* at divisions to present a cup or a shield or a set of medals; or else the captain was handing out his oak-leaves – the ship's own merit award – to inter-departmental champions.

That spring the *Royal Oak* carried off heavy-, welter- and feather-weight titles in the fleet boxing tournament, against competition from forty ships, and won the battleship hockey cup, beating the *Warspite*, the favourite, two-one. The rear-admiral came over one day especially to make the ship's company a congratulatory speech. He singled out the executive officer, Commander Wake-Walker, for particular praise.

The spring manoeuvres, the usual important and highly organised series of combined exercises with the Atlantic fleet, lasted three weeks and ended with a grand cavalcade of warships into Gibraltar bay. Scores of ships took part. 'The combined fleets,' wrote the midshipman, 'started to enter harbour at eight o'clock. Groups went in at short intervals and the last flotilla had not made fast until after five in the afternoon.' But everyone was rushing sports parties ashore the same day. The inter-fleet season was all too short to lose even an hour of daylight. The combined fleets' hockey eleven that drew with the Rock that night included three *Royal Oak* players.

Now it was the *Royal Oak's* turn to go home and re-commission. Sir Roger Keyes came on board at Gibraltar to wish her Godspeed and make special mention of 'the best thing she had done on the station' – not, as some of her crew thought, the thrashing she had just administered to the Atlantic fleet hockey champion, H.M.S. *Hood*, but a set of orders she had produced for a marines' striking force in a paper attack on a mythical beach.

The ship's paying-off pendant of cotton strips and bunting measured 650 feet – she had been in commission for 650 days. With the long streamer fluttering over her quarter-deck and the farewell cheers of the fleet sounding astern of her, she sailed for Devonport.

It was never the practice to keep the midshipmen on board during a long refit in a dockyard. Those who had not served a full term in the *Royal Oak* went back to Malta immediately and were distributed among the destroyers of the Mediterranean fleet until, in August, the battleship sailed once more into Grand Harbour. Rejoining her, the midshipmen found that she had been partly modernised (though the gunroom was as tight a fit as ever, perhaps tighter, with absurdly 'green' new boys from England); and that she had a new captain, William James, a future admiral.

The flag-officer came aboard soon after she returned. He had been administering his division from H.M.S. *Royal Sovereign* for the past three months, but she was now returning to the United Kingdom for *her* refit and recommissioning.

More changes were pending. After the second summer cruise, to the islands of the Dodecanese and the coast of Palestine and Asia Minor, the midshipman wrote:

'6th November 1927. At Malta. Boat-deck awnings were scrubbed. Captain Dewar arrived on board from England on Saturday morning and Captain James left on Sunday night, after watching the films of Coronel and the Falkland Isles. . . . All the officers were introduced to Captain Dewar. Our hockey team beat the *Barham's* three-nil.'

During her spell in Devonport dockyard the *Royal Oak* had acquired a cinema, one of the first to be fitted in H.M. ships in those most silent of silent days. The novelty of it was enough to keep the retiring captain on board twenty-four hours longer than he needed to be; or so it seemed to the diarist.

It was an important week for new arrivals and strange faces:

' 8th November 1927. The King of Spain paid an un-expected visit. He entered the Grand Harbour in the Spanish cruiser *Principe Alfonso* and was given a royal salute. She is one of the new class of 8,000-ton cruisers, of which three have been authorised. She was designed by Sir Philip Watts of Armstrong-Whitworth and was constructed at Ferrol dockyard under the supervision of British engineers . . . she was designed for 33 knots but has exceeded it on trials.'

' 12th November 1927. H.M.S. *Queen Elizabeth* arrived after her long refit in England. She has the new battleship top and bulges, a *Warspite* funnel, an extra tall mainmast with a special signalling position and very large bridges.'

' 13th November 1927. All officers were introduced to Rear-Admiral Collard, who came out in the *Queen Eliza-beth*. Divisions marched past him. The first rain of the year fell about nine o'clock in the evening.'

H.M.S. *Queen Elizabeth* had come back to wear the flag of the Commander-in-Chief and those ' very large bridges ' were made to accommodate the very large staff when she was at sea. The temporary fleet flagship, *Warspite*, now reverted to the rôle of flagship of the Admiral commanding the First Battle Squadron, Vice-Admiral John Kelly. He, too, was a comparative newcomer to the station. The day he came aboard the *Royal Oak* to inspect the ship's company and have the officers presented to him a tense but spectacular occasion was ruined by a sudden torrential downpour of rain.

These changes were all made in one hectic forenoon –

rendered even more hectic by the Commander-in-Chief's decision to bring tempers to the boil and nerves to breaking point as soon as possible by simultaneously exercising general drill – than which no item on the programme is better calculated to reduce a ship's personnel and material to chaos and set admirals, captains, commanders and first lieutenants at each other's throats. For the first time in months the *Royal Oak* suffered a mishap. She had laid out her stern anchor smartly enough in a race with her consorts, but when she came to hoist it in again from the launch alongside a strop parted and the seven-ton lump of iron fell back and dug its flukes through the bottom-boards of the launch. Quick thinking by the commander got the derrick rigged and the boat hoisted safely and it was back in the water, repaired, within twenty-four hours. But it had nearly killed three men and given the executive officer, Wake-Walker, and his new captain, Dewar, a nasty ten minutes.

It was very nearly the last service the ship's second-in-command performed for her. On Christmas Eve the midshipman jotted down details of another change among the senior officers – one of more significance for the gunroom and the lower deck than any other:

' 24th December 1927. Commander Daniel arrived in the s.s. *Khyber* and Commander Wake-Walker left the ship for England by the overland route.'

Everybody had an opportunity of inspecting the new admiral, captain and commander next day, when they made the time-honoured tour of the messdecks, to exchange the compliments of the season, admire the decorations and sip rum from a hundred proffered glasses and mugs. It was their first public appearance together. The admiral was a stocky, fiery little fellow with an impatient manner but a straight, piercing stare – the type one would not care to get on the wrong side of. The captain looked a cold, contemplative individual; not the kind to suffer fools gladly, either. But the new commander was exceptionally cheerful, lively and talkative, highly appreciative of the antics of the traditional ' funny party' that preceded the officers on their Christmas morning rounds.

Daniel was no stranger to some of the ship's company: they had known him on the station, in the *Barham*, and in the *Iron Duke* before her; known him as, above all, an enthusiast for entertainments. He was very quickly to give the word new meaning aboard the *Royal Oak*, starting with a children's party for sailors with families and friends ashore that opened the eyes of the most experienced and lavish organisers:

' There were slides, chutes, helter-skelters, various side-shows, a roundabout on the after capstan and a chair-lift to the upper conning tower. Elephants manned by officers were in constant demand as beasts of burden before tea. After tea the presents were captured by a highwayman from a coach and distributed to all the children by the Admiral and the Captain. During tea the " Oak Leaves " gave an entertainment and a cinema show concluded the party.'

The Commander played the highwayman. The ' Oak Leaves ' were the ship's concert party, acknowledged at that time to be one of the finest amateur companies ever seen on the station. Around the naval and military establishments and hospitals ashore at Malta they were much in demand at this season. Commander Daniel had already offered to write a sketch or two for them.

46

As things turned out, Captain Dewar's personality influenced the midshipmen's routine quite as much as Commander Daniel's. He was not at all like their previous captains, not a bit concerned about the inter-ship athletics meeting or the squadron squash competition. The only games that interested him were war games, played on the tactical board at the fleet educational centre, and he had all the subordinate officers up there twice a week for lectures and discussions on what most senior officers considered the 'forbidden' topics of strategy, tactics and policies. They were 'forbidden' because authority had laid down that only flag-officers were supposed to know anything about them; that discussion – after a fleet exercise, for example – by junior officers, the admirals of the future, might involve criticism of a senior officer's action, and that would be bad for discipline.

The Captain did not subscribe to these views. He devised situations on the tactical table to illustrate his theories, got the midshipmen to play them out and then asked for constructive suggestions. He made them write up accounts of the games in their journals and examined and initialled each one. He established a regular lecture programme: 'Conduct and Organisation of a Fleet,' by himself; 'Communications,' by Lieutenant Mountbatten (who had written a book on the subject and was writing another on polo, under the pseudonym 'Marco'); 'The Gunnery Problem,' by Commander Milford Haven.

As the gunroom advanced into realms of knowledge and thought, the existence of which they had barely suspected, they gradually retreated, and saw the rest of the 'Oaks' retreat, from the sporting limelight.

47

'Lost a hockey match against the Fourth Destroyer flotilla,' wrote the midshipman at the beginning of January 1928. ' We were beaten by the *Cardiff* in the marathon by about 200 points . . . the ship's rugby team lost sixteen-three against the *Barham's* in the semi-final of the battleship cup.'

CHAPTER IV

' A very capable officer '

THE three senior officers who came to join the *Royal Oak* as the year 1927 ended were to play leading parts in the most notable courts martial of the century, and to make the most talked-of contribution to the history of Sir Roger Keyes's reign in the Mediterranean – talked-of, but not much written about or discussed outside naval circles. To the layman, naval history means Jutland and Matapan, Trafalgar and the Glorious First of June; subjects not normally under review inside the Navy, except in library and lecture-room. Wardrooms and messdecks, when they take a backward glance, like to dwell not so much on the great milestones and turning points as on the incidents by the way – the bits of lore that have been reminisced into classics of naval *social* history, that would be fit themes for a ballad or chanty if sailors were nowadays that way inclined. The Archer-Shee postal-order case is one such incident; the Beresford-Scott controversy another; the Portsmouth ' mutiny ' a third, and the *Royal Oak* affair a fourth. To have been involved in one of these earns a naval officer a more positive immortality than if he had been awarded the Victoria Cross and made an Admiral of the Fleet. To have been involved in two, as Bernard St George Collard was, is unique.

Sail was dying when Collard joined the Navy – but not so fast that he was spared the grinding passage through the

mill of deliberate hardship that was a midshipman's life in
the eighteen-nineties. He learned what it meant to 'light
out to windward' on the weather yardarm, reefing topsails
for four long hours on a cold black night in a roaring Channel
gale (although a section of the press was to present him soon
as a spoiled brat who spent his adolescence drifting from one
floating gin-palace to the next).

Old-time conceptions of a fleet ponderously drilled and
administered by one master-mind on a bridge where
'captains spoke only to admirals and admirals spoke only to
God' (whose thought-processes were indeed as mysterious
as the Almighty's) were going out too. And so, as the
possibility of war clouded a distant future, were some
horrifyingly primitive hit-or-miss methods of naval gunnery.

H.M.S. *Dreadnought*, if not yet on the drawing-boards,
was narrowing into focus in her creator's mind. *Avant-
garde* notions about training young officers for specialist
duties, to advise their seniors and form a protective cluster
of expert opinions about him were circulating. The paths of
a Captain John Fisher, a Commander Percy Scott and a
Commander John Jellicoe were converging. They were all
three gunnery men and, if the day when gunnery was
acknowledged to be as important as paintwork was still far
off, the speed with which they rose to the top showed at
least where the most promising future for a specialist officer
lay. Gifted youngsters like Bernard Collard were in no
doubt about their choice of a branch when they completed
their sub-lieutenant's courses. They plumped for H.M.S.
Excellent, the naval gunnery school at Whale Island, Portsmouth.

Collard, the son of a Dorset clergyman, a shortish, well-

built young man with a rather severe and autocratic expression, had joined the Royal Navy from Clifton College
at the age of thirteen, and had spent the usual cadet's time
of two and a half years in H.M.S. *Britannia*, then an old
wooden hulk moored in the estuary of the river Dart. In
his first sea-going ship, on what was almost his first cruise,
Midshipman Collard had got himself noticed by saving a
sailor from drowning in the harbour at Aalesund, Norway.
In an age when sailors fell overboard with almost monotonous frequency and few could swim, rescuing drowning
men was a part of the daily routine for athletic young
officers; but Collard's act of bravery on this occasion had
been outstanding enough to earn him a special testimony
from the Royal Humane Society.

H.M.S. *Excellent*, where he came in 1899 to qualify, still
reverberated to the bark, gruff and explosive as a twelve-
pounder's, of bewhiskered old martinets flogging young
lieutenants through a course that turned them out as officers-
in-charge of a battery in a big ship or the whole armament
in a small one. There were ratings under instruction too,
potential seamen gunners or (a now-long-obsolete rate)
'captains of guns'.

The 'Island' promoted a training scheme that had
remained unaltered in essentials from Crimean days, a
scheme based on the watchword (only just beginning to be
regarded as slightly comical) that 'hattitude is the hart of
gunnery and whiskers make the man'. Admiral Sir
William James remembers these times:

'Classes of officers and seamen always moved about at the
double. The atmosphere was dynamic. I have seldom seen
such an exhilarating sight as a field-gun battery of eight guns

being drilled on the parade. Not the bat of an eyelid when at the halt and then, as orders were rapped out by an officer, marching, wheeling, shifting wheels with perfect precision. . . .'

What history calls the Gunnery Renaissance was shortly to be launched; some – by no means all – of the energy expended in stamping and shouting about the parade-ground would be diverted to the consideration of problems such as firing accurate broadsides into enemy warships at a little beyond point-blank range; and some of the gadgets Captain Percy Scott was inventing, or getting invented, for dramatically improving the percentage of hits while increasing the range at battle-firings, would go on test. Admiral James has recalled how the optical instrument firms, about this time, produced new and far better sights and range-finders, how the electrical firms began to supply reliable machinery for communicating between control positions and guns. Only then, he writes, 'was progress really accelerated. The improvement was indeed phenomenal. In a few years the range for battle-firings was extended from 5,000 to 23,000 yards, and torpedoes, which often ran crooked at 800 yards, were running straight at 10,000 '.

These were golden days of opportunity for alert young men in their early twenties, with good pairs of lungs and tastes for mathematics. The promotion path was wide and straight for those who got themselves taken on at Whale Island. The Navy was to choose many a future admiral from them. Collard was one.

When he finished the long gunnery course in 1901 he went, as the most promising graduates generally did, straight to the staff at Whale Island, to teach what he had just been taught. He was one of the last of the true 'gas and gaiters' school of instructors, one of those who had just finished their term of office and departed to sea when Captain Percy Scott himself became head of the 'Island', to sweep the place clean for the imminent Renaissance. Whale Island would suffer an invasion of scientists and strange devices. Its *curricula*, reshaped, would include abstruse subjects like gun-laying, sight-setting and director control and, as deeply entrenched 'barrack stanchions' gloomily forecast, the place would never be the same again. Science was getting a foothold in the gunnery fortress and the older breed of instructor scratched his head in bewilderment to hear foreign-sounding words like 'ballistic' and 'obturation' trip off the tongues of the newer breed of common sailor.

The newer breed: as the Navy changed, so did the boys who came forward to join it. So Collard found when he came home from sea to take up the job of senior gunnery officer at the Royal Naval barracks in Portsmouth, where one-third of all the 'new entries' in the Service reported. The change was not much to his liking.

Lieutenant Collard had been serving in the brand-new armoured cruiser *Drake*, under a powerful succession of captains who were to distinguish themselves in command of fleets one day: Bridgeman, Jellicoe and Sturdee. Now she was recommissioning as the flagship of Prince Louis of Battenberg.

The *Drake* had been a citadel of old-fashioned naval discipline and that was precisely what Collard was ordered to 'shake up' – that is, restore – when he came to the

barracks. Almost on his first turn of duty he found occasion
to. It was a dreary November evening in 1905. The fire
party was being mustered, a section of the duty watch – in
far too slapdash a fashion, Collard considered. He stopped
the roll-call and instructed the men to answer properly and
smartly in accordance with Service custom: " Here, sir,
please."

Soon afterwards a sailor named Acton answered, as
Collard later put it, ' very impertinently ' – he said simply,
" Here ". The lieutenant sharply corrected him and told
the petty officer in charge to call his name again, and again
Acton answered " Here ". At this, Collard was alleged to
have said, in a passion, " Go down on your knees, you dirty
dog, and learn your manners."

Acton was punished. Some weeks later a story began to
go round the barracks – and got into the *Daily Mirror* – that
he had been to see a solicitor, that the solicitor had been to
see Collard; and that Collard had paid over a sum of money
to hush the matter up.

A year passed before the officer himself had a chance to
nail the lie – and then he was appearing at a court martial
after a much more serious affair. " I have been attacked by
most of the halfpenny press throughout the kingdom for
things I have done and things I have not done," he said
indignantly, in his forceful, somewhat hoarse voice, " with
a virulence that I do not think anyone in my humble position
has ever before had to put up with. . . . I absolutely deny
having used any abusive words at all. I am not in the habit
of using abusive expressions when addressing men."

This was the aftermath of the celebrated Portsmouth
' mutiny '. The scene had once again been the parade-

ground at the Royal Naval barracks, the time once more a lowering November evening (exactly one year later), the villain, or hero (it was not yet clear which) once again Lieutenant Collard.

Hundreds of ratings were assembled for evening quarters – the last parade of the day. When it was done, while they were waiting to fall out, a heavy rainstorm suddenly swept the square. Some broke ranks and ran for shelter, the rest innocently followed. But Collard, the officer in charge of the parade, had given no order to dismiss and he instantly recalled them. After he had dismissed them formally, all the groups doubled away correctly, but a platoon of stokers was heard to mutter its disgruntlement as it went. Collard recalled the stokers a second time and started to lecture them – they were, he knew, mostly very new recruits. Perhaps deliberately, perhaps unthinkingly, but in any case not very wisely, he prefaced his remarks with the old-fashioned order: " On the knee ".

' Lieutenant Collard,' explained the *Hampshire Telegraph*, ' is a gunnery officer and it is an old standing practice in the Navy for a gunnery officer when addressing a party of men to order them to kneel upon one knee. The object of doing so is to ensure the officer seeing and being seen by all to whom he is speaking.'

The stokers did not see it like this. They thought they were being commanded to kneel to an officer and every one refused to obey. Collard gave the command again and again, and by force of personality got the whole contingent on its knees except for one man. He, with the inspiration of ' Uncle Tom's Cabin ' perhaps, declared to his Simon Legree that he would kneel before God and no one else.

Collard dismissed the stokers, spoke privately to the man and dismissed him also.

It should have been the last of the matter. It was a small affair. Not so very long before, sailors had been whipped into the rigging as a matter of routine, and the elderly midshipman with the warped sense of humour and the outsize feet whose dog-watch exercise was to get the sailors to come and lick his boots and then kick their teeth in had not long been dead. But in the barracks canteen at Portsmouth that night a sailor coming in drunk from the town mischievously roared out " On the knee! " – and in half an hour three hundred stokers and sympathisers had wrecked the building, broken all the glasses and bottles and streamed out across the flower-beds to the officers' quarters, bent on wrecking them too.

The alarm was sounded and the gates locked, the barracks guard standing to with fixed bayonets. The rioters, augmented by returning libertymen, almost all drunk, ranged through the barracks, smashing windows and furniture. It was early morning before the last was rounded up and the next night another outbreak of hooliganism took place. For Portsmouth, the hotbed of discipline and propriety, it was as though the millenium had arrived.

Lieutenant Collard took the blame for everything – blame that should have been apportioned, in the opinion of enlightened persons afterwards, between an ineffectual commodore and a slack commander, his superiors. Until the inevitable court martial he made no excuses and even then was careful not to incriminate anyone else.

The charges were (1) giving an unauthorised punishment (by ordering Acton to kneel to be told off); (2) using abusive language to a stoker; and (3) making improper use of the order ' On the knee '.

Some members of the court (Captain Henry Oliver of H.M.S. *Dryad*, the navigation school, was one, still alive and an Admiral of the Fleet in 1965) frankly admitted they had never heard of the order. Witnesses thought it came out of the old musketry drill-book. A petty officer remembered, years before, a whole battalion being ' put on the knee for fidgeting '. The petty officer in the Acton incident said he had never heard anyone give it to an individual until he met Lieutenant Collard. Collard himself, who knew all the drill-books and musketry manuals by heart, said it was still taught in H.M.S. *Excellent* and that *he* had been put on the knee, like his colleagues, more than once.

His firmness, self-confidence and unwavering calm impressed the court. They found him guilty on one charge only – that of giving the unauthorised punishment – and reprimanded him. " Don't take it too seriously," a sympathetic president privately advised him – advice that, taken in the literal sense, would have been helpful twenty years later. The affair was to do him no harm – excessive zeal and a too strict regard for discipline were, on the whole, admirable faults in an Edwardian naval officer, especially one with the task of introducing tough civilians to the harsh necessity of toeing the line. In its sequel it did him a lot of good.

The ' halfpenny press ' – the *Daily Mail* – had sent its brightest columnist down to Portsmouth to cover the ' mutiny '. He got the facts from the local correspondent and the human interest from sailors in public houses and produced one of the sensational, controversial stories for which he was becoming famous. His name was Edgar

Wallace. In a passionate plea for the rights of the underdog (he spoke with feeling, having been one himself not long before, in the South African campaign), he fumed:

' If men are treated like animals they will behave like animals. . . . It is a significant fact that four years ago Lieutenant Collard was involved in a similar case, which resulted in a court of inquiry, and in Lieutenant Collard losing six months' seniority.'

This was not true. And no sooner was he cleared of his court martial than Collard laid a complaint on the *Daily Mail*. Big newspaper actions for damages were in the fashion – Lever brothers had just taken fifty thousand pounds off Sir Alfred Harmsworth in a ' soap war ' libel suit, in which another imaginative creation of Edgar Wallace's, a mythical washerwoman, had largely figured. Harmsworth, particularly sensitive to the word libel, especially where his reporter whose pen ran away with him so often was concerned, hastily apologised. But this was not enough for the lieutenant. Early in 1907 he was suing for defamation of character. On 19th October he had the satisfaction of seeing a truly abject withdrawal of Wallace's remarks published in the *Daily Mail*; and a few days later he received a cheque for five thousand pounds, with which he built himself a nice country house, against the day, not far ahead now, when he would be getting married.

In the Royal Navy his stock went high: he had vindicated his honour and put the press in its place. His name, however, was said to have gone down in the little black book Harmsworth kept, joining the names of others with whom the future Lord Northcliffe intended one day to get even.

On one offender the *Daily Mail's* proprietor took immediate revenge. He had sent Wallace as far away as possible and now he sacked him. But the affair did Wallace a service too. It helped to set him up as novelist and playwright, for out of his detestable West African assignment came ' Sanders of the River '. Twenty years on, when Collard's name returned to the headlines, his chronicler at Portsmouth could afford sympathy: if not quite a millionaire he earned a millionaire's income. Traffic in the Strand halted to let his cream-coloured Rolls-Royce pass through, and people stood on chairs to get a glimpse of him when he entered the Carlton Grill for his lunch.

After the 1906 court martial, the Admiralty restricted use of the command ' On the knee ' to small-arms drill. In effect, they abolished it, and the Navy was to remember it for the future only as the nickname of that ' smart young officer, fated to attract notoriety ' as someone called him. The notoriety was vicious at times. When Collard went out to China, some of the Hong Kong shops had picture post-cards on sale against his arrival: doggy subjects, over-printed ' On the knee, you —— '.

Down in Portsmouth dockyard, a few hundred yards from the barracks where these incidents occurred, and almost next door to H.M.S. *Victory* within whose wooden walls the court martial had sat, more momentous affairs than the judgment of insignificant lieutenants were in hand. Within one year the most remarkable warship ever built, from a gunnery point of view, had been laid down and launched and was now fitting out, soon to commission. Lieutenant Collard had seen her ultra-modern superstructure rising on a skyline that was still a forest of wooden masts and yards.

During his time at the barracks he had often paid her a visit, to cast a keen professional eye over the turrets and main armament and unique control system that were going to revolutionise sea warfare. The production of H.M.S. *Dreadnought* was one of the earlier, but probably the most spectacular, achievements of the ' Fisher Era '. Sent back to Whale Island after the ' mutiny ', Collard stayed a year; played Rugby for the Navy; was selected to take a crew to Olympia, to pioneer that now-celebrated Royal Tournament event, the field-gun competition; and then went to the battleship *Glory* in the Mediterranean fleet, as first lieutenant and gunnery officer. He did well in her, and in 1909 he was made a commander (there being in those days no intermediate rank of lieutenant-commander) and got married. He was thirty-three, a comparatively early age in that period for acquiring either a wife or a brass hat.

Another major novelty Fisher and the twentieth century had presented to the Royal Navy was a War College, to which senior officers kicking their heels between appointments could go and reflect on, or debate, strategy, tactics, current affairs and such-like recherché topics. Collard took the course as part of his honeymoon before he went off to join the cruiser *Donegal* as second-in-command. Two years in the Atlantic fleet and three in the Naval Intelligence Division of the Admiralty in Whitehall took him up to the outbreak of the first World War.

Like everyone else in his department, he repeatedly requested to be shown some fighting. His turn came in the spring of 1915, when he was offered a job on the staff of the chief of operations in the Dardanelles and he saw fighting with a vengeance as assistant beachmaster at ' W ' Beach on the tip of Cape Helles throughout the landings and with-drawals. In June 1915, in the last promotions-list approved by the resigning First Lord, Winston Churchill, he became a captain – one of the youngest in the Navy.

Collard had been invalided home with a D.S.O. and a permanent limp, but within a few months he was back in action in his first command, the monitor H.M.S. *Lord Clive*. She helped to guard the Dover strait for more than two years, and Collard was still there when Rear-Admiral Roger Keyes (whom he had met at the Dardanelles on board the *Queen Elizabeth*) took command of the Channel forces to plug what had at last been recognised as gaping holes in the blockade.

At the armistice and throughout the period of the peace conference Captain Collard served at the Admiralty again, on the naval staff, and was appointed a Companion of the Bath for it. He was in the scarcely enviable position of Deputy Director of the Operations Division (John D. Kelly was its Director) when the German sailors scuttled their fleet at Scapa Flow. After a few months in command of the boys' training establishment at Portland, H.M.S. *Colossus*, he was recalled to the Admiralty to direct the Gunnery Depart-ment of the naval staff – a responsible job in which he was soon relieved by Captain F. C. Dreyer (who went out of his way to describe him as 'a very capable officer') in order to go to sea again and get in the necessary time qualification for promotion to flag rank. His first command was the destroyer *Valhalla*, a half-leader of a flotilla, and his second the battleship *Royal Sovereign* in the Mediterranean. In 1925 he was appointed A.D.C. to the King.

The piercing blue eyes of a true seadog stare out under

shaggy brows from a photograph taken about this time. Collard is thicker-set, more weather-beaten, more bulldog-jawed and seemingly shorter by now. His sleek dark hair is thinning out and the crows'-feet are deeply engraved at the corners of his eyes. Those who have fallen foul of him describe him as peppery, conceited and fussy. Those who know him better applaud his fairness and straight dealing, the uncomplicated rectitude of his views and decisions, the simplicity (and severity) of the code by which he gives and accepts orders.

' A tartar,' one of his sailors calls him, not unadmiringly. ' He couldn't half lay the law down.' To a commissioned gunner he appears ' a bit of an *enfant terrible* . . . got away with a lot, because he was Collard.' ' A stickler for discipline . . . " Whaley " from top to toe . . . frightful temper but with no malice with it . . . no time for slackers, arty types, " intellectual asses " as he called them ' – so his contemporaries (most of whom he had forged ahead of) saw him; in other words, a plain, old-fashioned firebrand of the type that made the British Navy, in the Edwardian era, the pride of the nation and envy of the world, a type that was perhaps only to be found in the Navy and even there was dying out. Physique, personality and personal courage had carried him triumphantly through forty years of naval life. When he came to the top of the captains' list in 1926 and was duly promoted rear-admiral, it could be confidently said that his prospects were as bright as any colleagues', that he might be safely tipped to reach the highest ranks of the Service.

After waiting about a year for employment, Rear-Admiral Bernard St George Collard, C.B., D.S.O., travelled out to the Mediterranean again to become the junior admiral in the First Battle Squadron. On the 7th November 1927 he hoisted his flag for the first time in the battleship *Royal Oak* at Malta. In selecting his staff, it was the choice of a flag-captain that gave him most thought. None that he would have chosen was available. In the end he accepted another ex-gunnery officer, Captain K. G. B. Dewar.

CHAPTER V

Renaissance and Reformation

ABOUT three years astern of Collard from the beginning, and following a surprisingly similar route through the well-charted but not always easily navigated channels of a naval career (Dartmouth, Greenwich, Whale Island, the fleet, the War College, the Admiralty and eventually command of a Mediterranean battleship) came Kenneth Gilbert Balmain Dewar. In H.M.S. *Britannia* he was a tall, fair-haired, good-looking cadet, quiet, studious and already introspective, a Scottish doctor's son with an elder brother a lieutenant in the Navy and a younger one to join after him (two of the three became admirals in due course, the third a captain). Before he arrived at Dartmouth, Dewar had been at the Collegiate School in Edinburgh, at Blair Lodge a few miles outside Edinburgh, and at a preparatory school in the Isle of Wight.

Dewar's first ship, in 1895, was the cruiser *Hawke* on the Mediterranean station. He was shortly transferred to the battleship *Magnificent*, second flagship in the Channel fleet, and then to H.M.S. *Volage*, a four-masted corvette of the training squadron. *Volage* was one of the last sailing war-ships and her captain a survival of the old, old Navy of hard-bitten eccentrics and originals. George Cherry figures in no naval history, but the Cherry medal had its place once in the dress regulations and is described in the older handbooks on

CAPTAIN K. G. B. DEWAR, C.B.E., R.N.

awards and decorations. Some of the captain's long-suffer-
ing officers instituted it, to give to anyone who managed to
last a full two-year commission with him. It bore the
stylised design of a cherry-tree with the rear view of a
retreating officer underneath it. The ribbon was black and
cherry red, and clasps were awarded to those whom the
captain had court-martialled but failed to break.

Dewar was not required to serve the full term. Promoted
lieutenant in 1901 and conspicuous for his cool, slightly
supercilious expression, he joined a torpedo-boat destroyer in
the Devonport flotilla and then, in the hope of seeing active
service while the war lasted, volunteered for abroad. 'War'
meant not the Boer war, which was in full swing nearer
home but passed almost unrecognised by the Navy, but the
Boxer rising in China, where the naval personalities of the
future were making names for themselves, names such as
Jellicoe, Beatty and Keyes. Dewar's promised appointment
to H.M.S. *Marathon* on that station came too late for him to
join in anything exciting, and he spent fifteen exhausting
months around Ceylon and the Persian Gulf in the hot little
coal-burning cruiser, under a commanding officer as peculiar
in his own fashion as Cherry had been.

'He was obsessed by certain theories concerning the
solar system', wrote Dewar, 'and I remember watching
him, assisted by his coxswain, tracing out cycloidal curves
on the white walls of the dockyard at Trincomali, to represent the paths of the planets through space. The procedure
was to lash brushes dipped in different coloured paints to
the spokes of a field-gun wheel at varying distances from the
hub and then rotate it along the wall. . . . One had to be
very discreet in asking questions, for the slightest hint of

doubt or criticism brought a flush to his face and a glint to his eyes. The "British blue", however, has his own opinion of his officers and the captain was far from unpopular on the lower deck. Every Sunday he gave the ship's company an harangue on some subject or other and I remember the men doubling aft eagerly to listen to it. On one occasion the captain found the sails of his galley dirty and the whole ship's company down to the cook was turned out to scrub them in the middle of the night. This was regarded as a really good joke and the men were roaring with laughter as they scrubbed the sails.'

The old cranky captains, whose tantrums made men's lives a misery yet who brought such colour to the deadly tedium of much of shipboard existence, were disappearing; but menacing mentalities remained – or so it seemed to Dewar. He was thinking of brains dulled and stiffened by a too-rigid code of instruction and conduct. Early training was as much at fault as anything, he decided: the *Britannia* 'caught little boys before they had learned to think and drilled them into a state of passive obedience'.

The marvellous appearance of H.M.S. *Hawke*, his first ship, pride of the Mediterranean fleet, could not fail to impress, with her funnel's glossy yellow, her upperworks' virgin white and the brilliant black of her hull. She was a product of the age when gunnery offered no serious challenge to spit-and-polish, when practically the whole of a crew's working day was occupied in housemaiding the ship, painting and dusting and scrubbing, when a battleship's commander went to the length of having the sheet anchor burnished for extra smartness and where a midshipman, if he wanted to get on, saved his pennies and twopences to buy a

66

brass boat-hook or extra cleaning rags or a ' tiddley ' mat for
the little boat he had charge of. Dewar remembered too,
behind that immaculate façade, the infestation and over-
crowding and disease in the living spaces; and the crimes
of violence, matched by punishment more violent, that
made sickening reading in the quarterly returns.

Seatime when he first went to sea meant manoeuvres,
little else. Day after day an admiral steamed his squadrons
to a selected square of ocean and there, like a sergeant-major
with his drill squad, put them through a series of quadrille-
like movements at constant speeds. No unexpected diversion was allowed to occur, no one else interfered with, or
got the chance to comment on, these perpetual and (to
Dewar) pointless waterborne square dances. Station-
keeping to a formidable degree of accuracy and instant
obedience to a monotonous series of orders were the only
requirements for captaincy. Individual ideas, individual
suggestions, individual resource and reasoning power
counted for nothing. It was disloyal as well as unnecessary
to think for oneself. If, as occasionally happened, a junior
admiral or captain found himself conducting a squadron or
flotilla into harbour after exercises he would be told, as often
as not, to take it out again and come in properly. It might
have been all right the first time, but this was the senior
admiral's way of reminding him, and showing the world,
who was really in charge.

Except for helping the ship's navigating officer in the
Magnificent to survey Pollenza bay (to which it would thereafter be an admiral's delight to bring his fleet in divisions,
several parallel lines, and carry out the celebrated simultaneous ' running moor ' with them), Midshipman Dewar

felt he had done nothing in his first four years at sea to render his career memorable. He knew, however, what he wanted to do; and once his sub-lieutenant's courses at Greenwich were over he applied for the long gunnery course at Whale Island and was soon under the command of the renowned Percy Scott.

Like Collard (then on the staff of H.M.S. *Excellent*, but not known to him) Dewar saw the old system of training vanish – without regret. He was forming and modifying his own opinions about naval education, and when the Custance committee invited representations about it from serving officers ten years later, Dewar would have plenty to tell them about the treatment of junior officers at Greenwich and on the ' Island '.

Reforming zeal and a conviction that, so often, all were out of step but himself made Dewar a rather lonely, independent figure throughout his career. He was put down as a disaffected, bumptious young know-all, ' arrogant and self-sufficient ', compensating for professional or psychological inadequacy by despising the system he could not measure up to. ' If he doesn't like things the way they are, why does he stay in the Service ? ' was the generally voiced reaction.

Time passed, and the Navy recognised him as a phenomenon: a young officer who thought things out for himself, with a rare talent for seeing the wood in spite of the trees – and a stubborn streak in argument. Academically he raced ahead of his class. No sour grapes prompted his strictures on the uselessness of the higher mathematics in the gunnery officer's curriculum, for example – he was top in mathematics. His marks earned him accelerated promotion, his ' independent thought ' lost him the *kudos* that went with it.

Captain Scott, principal *accoucheur* at the gunnery renaissance (whom Dewar admired), told the class in a lecture on modernising the ' Whaley ' traditions and techniques that he would welcome criticisms or suggestions. It was the first time Dewar had heard a captain ask a lieutenant's opinion about anything and he responded, on paper, in enthusiastic and forcible terms. The reply his instructor sent him ran:

' . . . I have received your paper. If you take my advice you will do well to use your pen as little as possible until you have gained a little more practical experience to season your theories, avoid controversy until your arguments are entitled to greater respect. When Captain Scott invited free criticism of his proposals it is hardly necessary for me to tell you that he did not ask for invective. You must learn that in the Public Service all communications from a junior to a senior are made in the submissive form and that all assertion is injurious to *both* sides. I have found it a very good rule in life *never* to put in writing over my signature anything that might be construed into presumption or anything that might be twisted into conflict with the public regulations and the Law of the Country. Diplomatic conciliation is worth oceans of the most highly justified dogmatism.'

From one twenty-two-year-old, or thereabouts, to another, this was not bad. It was the kind of thing Collard might have written – indeed, it must have been a fellow staff officer of Collard's who wrote it. Dewar kept the letter all his life – as a curiosity and an example of the hidebound stiffness he was complaining of. But it summed up a few of the rules that naval officers lived and prospered by and if, a quarter of a century on, the principals in the *Royal Oak* case had had them in mind, the careers of several prominent British sailors would have taken a different turning.

Early in 1903 Lieutenant Dewar joined the charmed and pampered world of the fully-fledged gunnery officer – charmed and pampered because, although it was already a cynical joke in the Navy that the only reason anyone became a gunnery officer was to avoid being shipmates with one, this was Fisher's Navy and for a few years at least the officer in charge of the ship's armament would be the aristocrat of her wardroom. Dewar's class at H.M.S. *Excellent*, and those before and after it in the early Edwardian days, were full of youngsters who would be admirals one day: James, Tudor, Fremantle, Domvile, Dreyer, Chatfield, Tovey and Fraser – this was only the beginning of a long list.

From Whale Island he went at once to his first command, the destroyer *Mermaid* – only for manoeuvres, to fill a gap, but the appointment was real distinction for all that. Most officers spent years negotiating for a command of their own. Collard had had to wait until he was a four-striped captain.

Later in the year, on the staff of the smaller gunnery school at Sheerness, Dewar began to 'teach himself to think', as he described it, putting himself under self-analysis and systematically repairing deficiencies in his general education – a most unusual step for a junior naval officer, all of whose training was directed towards producing the conviction that there were no deficiencies. His elder brother Alfred that year carried off the Royal United Service Institution's essay prize. K. G. B., finding himself attracted more and more to the intellectual side of his profession, saw no reason why he should not have a shot at something of the same kind himself.

But that had to wait. He was soon submerged in the mechanics of H.M.S. *Kent's* gunnery. She was an armoured cruiser with a lamentably inferior layout and no facilities for private study. When appeals for up-to-date armaments failed, Dewar neatly improvised and won the grudging approval of his new captain; which paved the way for a request to be allowed to give the crew a course of intensive training for the battle practice programme. This could never be, except at the cost of paintwork and polish. These were days when a battleship's turrets sometimes remained locked in the fore-and-aft position for the whole of a three-year commission, in case movement or firing of the guns split their high-gloss enamelling.

Dewar, never much concerned with personal popularity or slow to speak his mind, had many a memorable clash with the *Kent's* commander, once he had talked the captain round. The commander's promotion depended on bright-work, interference with *his* programme earned his implacable enmity. But the result was a magnificent performance by the *Kent* in Dewar's last year in her, in the 1907 series of battle-firings and gunlayers' tests. In those far-off days, little as gunnery was regarded by older officers set in their ways, all the nation followed the progress of the annual shoots. Newspapers carried round-by-round descriptions of ship, squadron and fleet performances. The whole of the Navy was listed in a kind of league table, and the public showed as much enthusiasm for the positions at the top as it did for the football championship or the fortunes of prize-fighters. Biographical studies and photographs of the officers, petty officers and seamen who made up winning teams frequently appeared in the press. For one day, when the 1907 results were announced and the *Kent* led the whole fleet, Britain rang with the names of Dewar and his party.

His picture of this date – he is in his late twenties – shows a slim, good-looking young man, the firmness of his mouth and chin softened by a dreamy expression of the eyes. He was not a typical sailor, in appearance, no bluff extrovert. Girls found him attractive ' in a serious kind of way ', says one who knew him then: ' – the sort of person you never felt you'd got through to '. Someone refers to his ' strange conversation, he took himself so seriously ' and someone else his ' sardonic, critical, obscure sense of humour '.

A naval officer averages two and a half years in each appointment – time enough to get to know the ship, and for the ship to get to know him. Dewar, quite fortuitously, had got off to a most unsettled start, with eleven ships in about eleven years. Now he joined a twelfth: the battle-ship *Prince George*.

Having achieved so much with an old ship's armament, and being something of a celebrity, he found it easier in the *Prince George* to claim the time and the resources her executive officer had traditionally regarded as his own. The captain particularly noted his new gunnery officer's talent for inspiring ' salt-horse ' (that is, non-specialist) lieutenants with a competitive fervour for drills. Lieutenant Dewar was broadening minds in all directions.

His plans for broadening his own received a jolt in the right direction when his ship visited Japan and he studied the work of the Japanese fleet and met Admiral Togo, hero of Tsushima, who represented for him the type of intelligent, independent-thinking sea commander the British Navy so desperately lacked. On return, he was paid the remarkable compliment for a junior officer of being invited to lecture the captains and commanders at the War College on his experiences in the land of the Rising Sun.

But when it was over, Dewar had the makings of another significant discourse on his experiences with the War College. He had told his audience a graphic tale of a Navy run on commonsense lines, where juniors were given responsibility and allowed to learn from their own mistakes, where admirals moved with the times and no one was penalised for candid comments . . . when the president of the College stood up and asked him to bring his lecture to a close. "The War College," he said, "is not the place to criticise the Admiralty." Dewar had overstepped the mark once more.

Where had he gone wrong? By failing to differentiate between fair comment and subversive criticism, it seemed. He had touched, he knew, upon topics about which the all-powerful Sir John Fisher was known to have strong views. Perhaps, he felt, on thinking it over, the War College dreaded listening to what the First Sea Lord would have considered heresy. They had invited a travelogue, and been given a tirade.

The president's subsequent action was hardly character-istic of the play-it-safe, stick-in-the-mud mentality Dewar credited him with. He circulated the script of the talk, after mild censorship, throughout the fleet, commending it to the attention of all officers as having something in it that was new and thought-provoking. Percy Scott, now a rear-admiral, sent Dewar his congratulations. The young man would be pleased to hear, he said, that in one cruiser squadron of the Royal Navy at least (the one he had the honour to command), a captain could ' blow his nose without asking permission '. Another Scott, of the *Bulwark* (soon, tragically for the Service, to be Scott of the Antarctic), wrote: ' Your criticism of our naval weaknesses is the ablest thing I have seen '. It is doubtful whether any young lieutenant ever had more striking testimonies paid by more celebrated seniors, to the power and originality of his ideas.

Early in 1909 (Commander Collard was arriving at the War College, just too late for the lecture), Dewar went to sea again, to his fourteenth job in as many years: gunnery officer of H.M.S. *Commonwealth* in the Channel fleet. Again he mourned, to anyone who would listen, the deadly monotony of a life controlled twenty-four hours a day by signal from the flagship. Again he saw captains and squadron admirals, one day perhaps to be Commanders-in-Chief themselves, denied the exercise of initiative and ' independent thought' because they could do nothing but conform to the Commander-in-Chief's movements. The follow-my-leader fetish ruled the simplest areas of domestic shipboard life: when it came on to rain, Dewar's captain dared not allow his officer of the watch to slope awnings until the flagship ordered all ships to slope awnings; when the rain stopped, before any ship made a move to dry up decks she waited for the flagship to signal ' Dry up decks '. The march of naval progress was not a march in any particular direction, just a matter of marking time in step.

Gunnery, the gunnery officer noted, after eight years now of new brooms and alleged clean sweeps all round, was still largely associated with ' everyone rushing about the ship accompanied by the clash of securing chains and slamming of breech-blocks, much to the detriment of delicate gun mechanisms'. He went for a spell on the staff of the Inspector of Target Practice and toured the various fleets, comparing their shooting efficiency. One of the minor problems Percy Scott had never resolved was how to cut out the time-wasting re-erecting of targets during battle practice. Dewar produced a do-it-yourself scheme for ship's companies that saved hours. Of his tour of the fleets, he left it on record that ' the shouters on parade who get worked up about gunnery are not often great successes at hitting the target ' – one in the eye for the ' gas and gaiters ' robots, of whom there were still far too many about.

Quite the most coveted appointment for a gunnery lieutenant in later Edwardian days was to the floating wonder of the western world, H.M.S. *Dreadnought*, wearing the flag of the Commander-in-Chief Home Fleet. Dewar got it, in January 1910. He became gunnery officer and first lieutenant, and although he found much to complain of in Fisher's brain-child (the funnel perfectly sited to smother the main control position in smoke, the view from the conning tower effectively masked by stanchions and rigging) he found himself in congenial company. William Words-worth Fisher (a future admiral) was her unconventional, popular and energetic second-in-command. Herbert Rich-mond (who ended his active career as president of the Imperial Defence College) was her captain – a historian and strategist and rebel, a patron of ' independent thought ' and from this time onwards a friend, collaborator and supporter of Dewar throughout his life.

Captain Richmond's impatience with his Commander-in-

Chief (whose friend and flag-captain he was supposed to be) overflowed the pages of his diary and communicated itself to his intimates. He thought the Navy's hope lay in thoughtful young officers not yet infected by the ' tactical arthritis ' that afflicted the admirals. One day he invited half a dozen lieutenants – Dewar among them – to his home at Alverstoke to talk about forming a club to stir up interest in subjects like the principles of war, which senior officers monopolised. Out of the meeting came the idea for a *Naval Review*, a journal that would express ' independent thought ' by anyone, however junior, provided it was to the point. The first issue was financed by Richmond and his ' set ' – a ' set ' of which Dewar was a prominent member and which was to be disliked and mistrusted by most of the admirals. Today the *Naval Review* is a respected organ of Service opinion, but authority frowned on its birth.

Richmond got Dewar his promotion. He himself died an admiral, but, although Commander-in-Chief East Indies before going to the Imperial Defence College, he never knew the honours his talent should have qualified him for, never led out on manoeuvres the fleets he deployed in such masterly fashion on paper. Ironically, mention of his name to most naval officers recalls only the ' Abyssinian princes ' hoax that made the *Dreadnought* (and the Navy) the laughing-stock of a season. Lieutenant Dewar was also involved: he showed the practical jokers round the turrets and delayed the sunset ceremony on the quarter-deck until their own interminable and altogether spurious evening ritual with prayer-mats and incantations was done.

On leaving the *Dreadnought*, Dewar became a Commander (he was only thirty-one) and joined the staff of the War College. If he thought a brass hat and a staff appointment would entitle him to lay down the law more successfully than before, he was early disillusioned. The director impressed on him from the start that ' commanders confine themselves to facts and do not offer opinions. Only admirals are supposed to know anything about tactics or strategy or methods of command '. He passed much of his time in the library, consoled when the Royal United Service Institution awarded him its 1912 gold medal for an essay describing how the fleet ought to blockade northern Europe in the forthcoming war – how, more or less in fact, the fleet eventually did.

Armageddon 1914 found Dewar newly married and second-in-command of H.M.S. *Prince of Wales*, a flagship in the Channel fleet. At Sheerness he cut himself shaving when the *Bulwark* blew up just along the river in one of the catastrophic mysteries of the first World War. Early next year the *Prince of Wales* was in action herself, at the Dardanelles. Dewar (like Commander Collard, a mile or so away) saw 'heroism, hard work and suffering . . . muddle, mismanagement and useless sacrifice'. Once a gunnery officer, always a gunnery officer, he could not resist writing privately to his squadron admiral – though it was no longer his business – to suggest a more intelligent method of controlling the shore bombardment.

His old captain, Richmond, was out there too, as a liaison officer with the Duke of Abruzzi's Italian forces. Dewar sometimes went ashore to meet him and take a walk over the northern Aegean hills and work off his frustrations with anecdotes about the prevalence of red tape in the battle area.

Admiral Keyes, in the flagship *Queen Elizabeth*, thought the Gallipoli operations should never have been abandoned. Dewar believed they never should have been started. After what he called the 'desperate and unjustified gamble' failed he went home, first to spend a few months in charge of the Gunnery School at Devonport (where he was specially mentioned for zeal, tact and ability) and then to a seagoing ship of his own. It was the *Roberts*, a monitor, like the one Collard was running at Dover. These ships, slow, lumbering, floating shore batteries, stationed up and down the coast and camouflaged to look like clumps of trees and public houses, were something of a joke in the war. Dewar was based on Lowestoft and saw no action worth speaking of. It was at the Admiralty, where he went next, that his real battles were fought.

Lord Jellicoe, now First Sea Lord, summoned him in 1917 to write a weekly appreciation of the war at sea for the Cabinet. The job did not last long; Dewar was often in hot water – for publishing the truth about shipping losses, he claimed, and 'giving the politicians too much ammunition'. An objectionable appointment was his reward, command of an antiquated cruiser in the East Indies. He protested officially and, to be on the safe side, got in touch with a friend of the Prime Minister. Lloyd George had a weakness for listening to gossip from junior officers; from Captain Herbert Richmond he had heard home-truths about the admirals, and it was perhaps Richmond who mentioned Dewar's name. The latter found himself one day having lunch at 10 Downing Street and giving Lloyd George his views on the convoy system, Jutland and the war of succession among the Sea Lords – this at a time in the nation's affairs when the First Lord himself pleaded in vain for a five-minute chat with the Prime Minister.

Further back, the man who had mentioned Richmond's name was one of the sailors who had retired to enter Parliament and bring pressure to bear from the back benches of a kind serving officers never dreamed could be applied. He was Commander Carlyon Bellairs, a Parliamentarian of such seniority that he could have been excused for having degenerated into a garrulous old windbag; in fact he was wide-awake, keen and voluble, and the acknowledged expert on naval affairs, although his active service had abruptly ended, because of failing eyesight, about the time of Queen Victoria's death. He had been shipmates in the nineties with Herbert Richmond, who could consider his own comparative unpopularity with some members of the Board of Admiralty more than offset by his friendship with so influential an M.P. ' Do what St Vincent did – skip all the admirals and dive down to the captains' list. You'll find Richmond there,' Bellairs had breezily informed Sir Eric Geddes when the new First Lord had asked him to suggest a suitable successor for Jellicoe!

Shortly to join Bellairs in the House – on the opposite side – was Lieutenant-Commander Joseph Kenworthy, who had entered the Navy about the time Bellairs left it and was now retiring to contest Kingston-upon-Hull in the Labour interest. When matters associated with shipping and the sea, however remotely, were under debate, Bellairs over the next decade or more was to play Scylla to his equally loquacious opponent's Charybdis; and many were the innocent craft steered by post-war First Lords that were to be spectacularly demolished by the one while running to avoid the other.

Commander Kenneth Dewar, his foreign appointment cancelled, went from one Admiralty department to another. A Plans Division, for which the *Naval Review* had been shouting, was eventually set up with Captain Dudley Pound as its director. He chose Dewar for an assistant. The Division expanded and its staff proliferated. Soon it needed a rear-admiral at the head. Roger Keyes filled that post and, attracted to him by a common dislike of Jellicoe, kept Dewar on and even recommended him for promotion. But as long as Jellicoe remained First Sea Lord there was little hope – he liked neither Keyes nor Dewar, considered both too full of bright ideas. It was June 1918, and Jellicoe had gone, when Commander Dewar surmounted the next hurdle. It made him, at thirty-nine, as it had made Collard three years earlier, one of the youngest captains in the Royal Navy.

A clash with Lord Beatty, just before the war ended, earned Dewar a mention and a footnote in the *Official History*. The young captain from Plans, on a visit to the Grand Fleet, was told about the risks the Scandinavian convoys were being made to run.

'A few weeks later', says the *History*, 'both Admiral Fremantle (Deputy Chief of the Naval Staff) and Captain Dewar had reason to remember the Commander-in-Chief's warning'.

A convoy had narrowly escaped destruction by the German fleet. Dewar took exception to the implied slur and made such tenacious efforts to get his name deleted from the passage that a note was inserted:

' The conversation (with Lord Beatty) was quite unofficial. Captain Dewar was in no way responsible for the existing arrangements.'

He was among the naval contingent that travelled to Paris for the peace conference to represent Britain's views on President Wilson's ' freedom of the seas' point. He received the C.B.E. after Versailles, but the highlight of the expedition, for him, had been an introduction to Lawrence of Arabia, perhaps the most successful exponent of ' independent thought' then living.

The war was won and lost. But at the Admiralty the fighting went on. The signing of the peace treaties brought no peace of mind to Captain Dewar. He had fastened on a job at the Staff College and been told, when everything was as good as settled, that ' unexpected difficulties' had arisen. An argument with the Second Sea Lord led to his being ordered to another period-piece cruiser, this one lying forgotten in some Black Sea port few had ever heard of. For the second time in his career he refused an appointment and for the second time won his fight. On top of all this the *Naval Review* got out of its depth. It published a fault-finding article about Sir Berkeley Milne and his chase of the *Goeben*, and the Board of Admiralty ruled that, although the journal was privately circulated, future issues must be censored beforehand.

' Sir, I have the honour to submit—.' Dewar's brother had retired and now Dewar himself, with *fin-de-guerre* disillusionment, was going to do the same. On second thoughts, he decided to ask for a year's unemployed time, to consider his future. But before that was up the Admiralty invited him back – along with his brother – to prepare the official account of the Battle of Jutland.

It was to occupy him for the best part of the next two years, and to turn out a thankless task. If the Dewars had friends before they began, those friends were fewer after they finished. Too many Jutland veterans were still alive, still engaged in a longer running fight, the promotion battle, still anxious to clear their individual yardarms after the action.

Five difficult years in and around Whitehall ended for Kenneth Dewar with a new appointment that was as much to his liking as any could be: commanding officer of H.M.S. *Calcutta* and later of H.M.S. *Capetown*, both smart new light cruisers on the West Indies station. Each ship, for a short period, wore the flag of the Commander-in-Chief.

Captains of warships, especially larger warships, inevitably give the impression of being rather hermit-like creatures. Dewar, in the recollection of former ships' officers of the period, seemed more of a recluse than most. ' Made little impact ' . . . ' appeared to view the activities around him with a kind of ironic detachment ' . . . ' remained quite unknown to, and unseen by, a proportion of the crew '. The colours in which his subordinates paint him differ from one to another, but all are hazy and indistinct. ' I suppose I must have seen him,' says one, who spent ten months in the *Capetown*, ' but I couldn't tell you what he looked like.' One officer claims he was not once spoken to by the captain between the two formal shakes of the hand on joining and leaving; an ex-midshipman, whose duties brought him into more frequent contact than most, said the captain always treated him like a complete stranger and, after six months of it, was still calling him by the wrong name.

Yet Dewar took more interest in the midshipmen than most captains were able or willing to. He instituted a series of lectures and readings and debates, covering what he called the 'higher branches of naval knowledge' – strategy and tactics, of course, plus conduct of a fleet in war and peace, the training of officers, the staff system, the shaping of the Navy to come – all the subjects his mind had ranged over for so long, that had brought him into conflict with conventional thought so often.

'The seed', he wrote, of this scheme, 'fell on very stony ground'. The bright young men, fresh from Dartmouth, displayed 'an astonishing incapacity for independent thought'.

When he came back to England in 1924, the job he had set his heart on seemed within his grasp: the directorship of the Staff College was about to fall vacant. One of the bitterest disappointments of his life was to be told that private means were now essential for this post, entertaining having become the most important side of the director's duties (a tactful way of putting it: Dewar would have turned the place upside down). 'My thoughts went back to the War College days of 1912 and 1913', he wrote, 'and I remembered how the strategical exercises were based on blockading the Heligoland bight and tactical games on the rigid single line. Neither private means nor entertaining is likely to guard us from similar mistakes in the future'.

Instead, the Admiralty once more. One imagines a cry going up, 'Dewar is back!' – for few officers of his age could have spent more time there. Now it was the Naval

Intelligence Division. He was its Deputy Director – ' one more bottleneck in the stream of papers passing round ', as he disgustedly described himself. He whiled away the time worrying his chiefs, first Admiral Hotham and then his old *Dreadnought* colleague, W. W. Fisher, about streamlining the department and cutting down what the First Sea Lord, Beatty, described as ' the game of dockets' that was endlessly played in and out of the offices.

His two years up, Dewar accepted the appointment of flag-captain to Rear-Admiral Bernard Collard in H.M.S. *Royal Oak* in the First Battle Squadron of the Mediterranean fleet. Neither was inclined to throw his oak-leaved cap in the air about the arrangement. Collard, unable to exercise his traditional privilege of choosing his own flag-captain, because none of his friends was currently available, took Dewar to do him a good turn because the latter was close to the top of the captains' list and needed more sea-time to qualify him for promotion to rear-admiral. Except for chance meetings over the years – mainly at the Admiralty – Collard hardly knew the man, He knew all about him: his ' independent thought ', which was another way of saying ' bolshie ideas '. He had been warned that Dewar was not everyone's choice as the perfect subordinate.

For his part, Dewar wanted a private ship – that is, a ship unencumbered by admirals. He did not care to ask for one because he was no more *persona grata* with the latest First Sea Lord, Sir Charles Madden, than he had been with Jellicoe ten years before. In their *Narrative of the Battle of Jutland* the Dewar brothers had rapped some admirals of the Jellicoe faction with more smartness than tact. Madden had been chief of staff on board the *Iron Duke* in that encounter and could not get the *Narrative* out of his head. ' But as soon as he became First Sea Lord he quickly got it out of circulation ', says Dewar, ' by calling in all copies and committing them to the flames '.

As to the flag-officer who came along with his new command, Dewar was not particularly looking forward to serving him. All he heard about Collard – his impatience and irascibility, his fondness for a party, his popularity with the lower deck but not, it was reputed, with the wardroom, his ' gas and gaiters ' mentality – confirmed what he instinctively felt: that they were not likely to be a really well-matched team.

Mutual acquaintances of them both, seeing the announcement in the naval columns of the press, shook their heads to see two such diametrically opposed temperaments brought so inescapably together; two pig-headed gunnery officers, holding clashing opinions; two who were famous for speaking out of turn – all the ingredients for an explosive mixture were here. The *Royal Oak* was now to hold the fatal combination that had brought trouble to the *Resolution*: Collard was a junior admiral, as Staveley had been; Dewar a senior captain, like Martyn. And bitter animosity had characterised the Staveley-Martin partnership, injurious to both. Another flag-officer in Malta, with whom Dewar took a stroll ashore the night he arrived and to whom he aired his views about ' being dictated to ', privately forecast another row in the squadron. He gave them both–Collard and Dewar–about three months.

But Roger Keyes and ' Joe ' Kelly were there; after the last spot of bother they would be keeping a wary eye on things. Collard, the rumour went, had changed a lot, grown meek as a lamb, since he got his flag. Dewar, surely, had too much to lose to make trouble at this stage? It was only for a year, after all.

Kenneth Gilbert Balmain Dewar spent the first few days after his arrival in Malta walking round the *Royal Oak* and paying and receiving the many formal calls that regulations demanded of a new captain on the station; and in poring over the library of standing orders and memoranda that his predecessor had left him. It was some years since he had served in a big fleet and the apparent top-heaviness of the administrative structure appalled and saddened him. To one who had been brought up in the era of truly grand fleets, the Mediterranean fleet at that moment was certainly not impressive in tonnage: seven battleships, twelve cruisers and thirty-two destroyers. But in the fleet flagship alone he counted thirty-one 'passengers' – officers with no ship's duties, solely engaged on staff work for the Commander-in-Chief. Nor was that the whole tale: on top of that, Vice-Admiral Kelly had a staff of twelve to administer the Battle Squadron – six ships; and his own Sammy Collard (he was 'Sammy' these days, one never heard 'On the knee') – Sammy Collard, due to join any day now, was proposing to maintain a staff of four in the *Royal Oak*, although he would have no command of any kind, in the strict sense of the word.

Dewar did not at all care for the idea of a huge administrative staff in the *Queen Elizabeth* superimposed on another in the *Warspite*, both heaped on top of a third in the *Royal Oak* and all three interfering with the responsibilities of her commanding officer. Whitehall had taught Dewar to recognise bureaucratic empire-building when he saw it, and he could not help feeling he was in for a bad bout of tactical paralysis in the Mediterranean fleet.

About the *Oak* herself, the ' Mighty Oak ' as the sailors called her, he had no misgivings. Not a ' big ship ' man by nature, he could nevertheless not fail to congratulate himself on having achieved a truly impressive command. To be captain of a battleship on the Mediterranean station – a ship about six times the size of anything he had commanded before – made Dewar an almost regal personage in Malta. To be respectfully saluted by tradesmen, gazed at in awe by Maltese youth, worshipped by servants and revered by dghaisamen was a heart-warming experience both for the captain and his wife (Mrs Dewar had travelled out to live ashore in Malta), fresh from a Great Britain that was somewhat gloomily and uncertainly recovering from the General Strike.

The ship's sporting stock stood high, her chances in the forthcoming annual gunnery competition seemed good, she had a reputation for being friendly and hospitable. And this was not a sign that her wardroom was full of those butterflies and self-seekers whose interests and ambitions revolved round cocktail parties at Admiralty House or horsy doings at the Marsa. He had a good team of officers. Just one, and no more, had been a member of the fast polo-and-racing crowd and, if Dewar had anything to do with it, there would be no more. He carried one staff officer for the squadron, additional to those the rear-admiral would be bringing. This was the squadron navigating officer, a quiet, serious-minded commander, who would be president of the wardroom mess as soon as the admirably business-like Wake-Walker, the ship's executive officer, went home.

Wake-Walker's relief was to be another brightish ex-gunnery officer, H. M. Daniel. Dewar knew him, or knew of him, as one member of the ' Branch ' knows, or knows of, another. He had, in fact, already had him as one of his officers for a week or two, while Commanding Officer of the Devonport Gunnery School, but could not remember what he looked like. Commander Daniel would have little to learn about protocol and procedure in Malta and in the Battle Squadron, he knew that much; for the new executive officer had been out here, more or less continuously, in different battleships for the past five years.

CHAPTER VI

Tactical Advantage

THIRD of the trio whose collision was to rock the British fleet with the violence of a white squall in a tropical anchorage, Henry Martin Daniel (like Collard the son of a country clergyman) joined the *Britannia* a few years after Dewar and first went to sea in the battleship *Bulwark* about the time of the Portsmouth ' mutiny '.

The morning on which she blew into fragments in the Medway estuary, within earshot of Dewar, was still nearly a decade away. During Daniel's midshipman's time in her she was wearing the flags of successive Commanders-in-Chief in the Mediterranean – Sir Compton Domville and the legendary Lord Charles Beresford. In 1909, just before Captain Robert Falcon Scott took command of her, Daniel went ashore for the usual courses and was then appointed, as sub-lieutenant, to another battleship and flagship in the Home Fleet: H.M.S. *Lord Nelson*, flagship of Rear-Admiral Doveton Sturdee. His third sea-going appointment was to yet another battleship, under the captaincy of yet another Commander-in-Chief-to-be, Frederick Field. Seven years – the melting-pot years – under officers with great names like these, whose notations on a subordinate officer's confidential reports carried weight that had its effect throughout one's career, got Daniel off to a flying start.

When his chance came to specialise, he chose gunnery – or

rather, was chosen, because as in Collard's and Dewar's time the branch was largely composed of a hand-picked élite. The renaissance was over, the golden age of naval gunnery had arrived, Whale Island after Percy Scott had finished with it as unrecognisable to habitués of the early nineteen-hundreds as it had been in their time to habitués of the eighteen-nineties. Daniel was undergoing the long course there in 1914 when war broke out; completing it in time to go to sea and spend almost the whole of the period of hostilities afloat on active service.

Except for his wartime appointments, Daniel spent all his seagoing career in battleships. But from 1914 to 1919 he was gunnery lieutenant of a light cruiser, first the *Isis* and next the *Royalist*, partly in the Harwich force and partly in the Grand fleet; and then the *Dauntless*, one of the latest of her kind, in Admiral Cowan's Baltic Squadron. Each of these ships, though not much in the public eye, steamed more miles than most and was constantly engaged in sweeps and forays and perilous undertakings. Their reputations – and preservation – depended on their gunnery lieutenants, who were all carefully selected. Daniel was noted among his colleagues for devotion to duty, force of personality and exemplary calm under stress. In H.M.S. *Royalist* he was mentioned in despatches.

The *Dauntless* served in Russian waters after the Armistice for the two-hundred-day 'war' against the Bolshevists. Her task was to preserve the blockade of Libau against German shipping, and support the advance of the Esthonians up the coast towards the Gulf of Riga; to support anybody, in effect, who showed enough spirit to resist the Red Navy and Red Army. Bombardment of islands and of the coastline was a necessary feature of the campaign, with plenty of hot work for gunnery officers. There was an operation in which the *Dauntless* was concerned where, for three days, Cowan's forces pounded an unseen target without a hit, until Daniel landed secretly by night on the enemy shore and set up an observation post from which to spot the fall of shot and send back semaphored corrections: a courageous adventure, skilfully conceived and carried out, entirely his own idea, for which he got the D.S.O.

From the *Dauntless*, in 1920, he joined the modern battle-ship *Valiant* as first lieutenant and gunnery officer. Out of this commission nothing memorable came, except a small but elaborate publication written by himself, entitled ' H.M. *Valiants* ' – a prose and pictorial record of all the warships that had borne the name. He achieved the expected promo-tion to Commander, a little in advance of his contemporaries, and returned to the Admiralty in 1922, to spend the next four years all but a few months in the Naval Ordnance Department – writing another book; but this was a tech-nical manual on gunnery, a large, detailed and intricate work that is regarded even today as a model of its kind.

Daniel was a tall, pleasant-looking person – in spite of, at this period, thinning hair, deep-set eyes and a rather har-assed, jumpy expression. He gave the impression of positively bursting with energy – athletic, with a few endurance feats to his credit, but with none of the relaxed off-duty languor that so often marks the real top-class athlete. Someone said that ' mercurial ' best described his temperament – moody, manic, seized with sudden enthusiasms, forcible in word and action (but straitlaced too, a Christian Scientist and man of principle), one day hail-fellow-well-met, talkative and amusing, the next sulky and withdrawn, impatient with his colleagues and monosyllabic. Daniel would never conform to the conventional portrait of the British naval officer. Apart from anything else, he was suspected of having ' arty ' tendencies – suspected but not condemned for it, because he had proved himself by writing books and was a useful hand at playlets and sketches for concert parties and the like.

' Hated bawling people out ', a contemporary recalled. ' But a bit inclined to go off at half-cock ', is another's qualification. ' An absolute charmer, when he liked to be ' – ' Sometimes you couldn't get a civil word out of him '. A person, clearly, of contradictions.

An officer in H.M.S. *Iron Duke*, in the Mediterranean, to which Daniel was sent as gunnery commander on the vice-admiral's staff in 1925, was impressed above all with the way he ' frantically busied himself, twenty hours a day: always doing something, and doing it flat out – not always the right thing, however '. But he ' knew his stuff – easily the smartest squadron gunnery officer we had had up to that time '.

When the old battleship went home, Commander Daniel transferred to the *Barham*, and, on being relieved by Lord Milford Haven, went almost at once to another battleship in the adjoining berth in Grand Harbour (by way of England, for a few days' leave). She was the *Royal Oak* and he was to be her commander – a job that would assure his further promotion, barring accidents, at a fairly early date.

Daniel had now served a long term on the station, and the social set – wives, ' fishing fleet ' and civilians ashore – long remembered him; for his was the inspiration behind some of the outstanding leisure attractions. His treasure hunt in the *Barham* was voted the event of the season, and set the pattern for what was thereafter to become an essential feature of the entertainments the Navy provided for its friends and visitors. There was a magnificent ball in the *Iron Duke* while she was flagship at Malta, that very nearly made her more of a celebrity than she had been after Jutland; Daniel was the sole organiser and impresario, the leader of the ship's sporting and social life, besides being, as every executive officer in a battleship must be, the busiest sailor on board.

Aged ex-bright-young-things speak nostalgically still of the grand fancy dress affair on board two of the Mediterranean battleships, berthed side by side for the occasion. 'The Commander simply excelled himself over this; it was the party to end all parties, as far as Malta was concerned. He very modestly went as " *Die Fliedermaus* " and spent the whole night spreadeagled upside-down on the ceiling . . . then he got his gunnery reports late, or something, and got into frightful trouble over it. Always trying to do so much.'

Professionally, he scored some excellent hits for all that. Two years running his organisation for the competitive battle-firings was the pride of the ship, the envy of fellow gunnery men, the admiration of the fleet and the subject of a special commendation from the Commander-in-Chief.

When Roger Keyes launched the era of furious activity at Malta, Daniel was more furiously active than most. When not concerned in schemes for making a name for the ship – and himself – in seamanship and gunnery, or dreaming up original stunts for parties and pastimes, he was writing a novel, or a play, long into the night, or flinging himself into some cultural venture that had – perhaps only momentarily –

caught his attention. Elected to the committee of the Malta Amateur Dramatic Club, he fell out with the rest of the members when they declined to put on a three-act comedy he had dashed off in the first flush of excitement for theatricals. 'You never read such pretentious stuff', the then producer, a captain of one of the Mediterranean destroyers, wrote. An elderly lady on the island, at that time one of the Club's *ingénues*, confirms, sadly and sympathetically, that it was a 'dreadful play'. She offended the author by telling him, as tactfully as she could, that she could not see herself in the part he had earmarked her for; 'Henry Daniel took it very sulkily indeed' – and scarcely ever spoke to her, or to the producer, again.

These were critical times for Daniel, of course. He was now in a run of 'promotion jobs' and ultra-conscious of it. Overworked and hypersensitive he may have been but, by all accounts, he at least refrained from working off his tensions on the junior officers in the *Royal Oak*, who came under his authority. 'We all loved the Commander', wrote one of them, ' – he could so easily be *bounced*'. Unlike his predecessor, the tyrant Wake-Walker, who had ruthlessly dragged the ship to a high state of technical efficiency (and left some bruised egos behind him), Daniel in the short few months he had in the *Royal Oak* seemed to get much the same output with a mixture of what was then called 'jollying' and appeals to a sense of fair play and a lot of personal endeavour and example. An able seaman described him, privately and uncompromisingly, as 'wet – you could have scrubbed the quarter-deck with him'. But the anecdote he adduced as evidence was really a measure of the concentration Daniel brought to any job he tackled, big or small: the seaman was painting the ship's after screen when the Commander came by and told him what a poor fist he was making of it; took the brush to demonstrate and became so absorbed in the job that he finished it – while the sailor stood grinning at his side, admiring the scenery and occasionally condescending to point out bits the perfectionist had missed.

As the midshipman's journal recorded, Commander H. M. Daniel, D.S.O., joined the *Royal Oak* on Christmas Eve, 1927. His predecessor, Wake-Walker, left at once – and was promoted captain as soon as he arrived home (he ended up as Third Sea Lord). Captain Dewar had now commanded the ship for nearly two months, Rear-Admiral Collard's flag had streamed from her maintop for not quite so long. Three gunnery specialists who (to recall the old jibe) had qualified in order to be spared ever serving with another of their kind, had all come together at last. The principal actors were assembled. Henry Martin Daniel, characteristically plunging in, alive with enthusiasm, to Christmas and New Year festivities – children's parties, concert parties, revels of all kinds to suit a hundred tastes – lost no time in regrouping the ship's various social committees and voting himself into their chairs. Much of the donkeywork attached to the organisation of the forthcoming wardroom dance he took upon his own shoulders. He was setting the scene for the first act in the *Royal Oak* drama: a first act of such awe-inspiring triviality as would have tempted him, had he been writing the play himself, to tear the whole thing up and start again.

For the landsman, at the best of times, there is a mystery and a foreignness about naval personnel. Sailors belong to a monastic order, the incomprehensible rules of which are uninfringed by all the hospitality they dispense to strangers on board their ships, even on a station so highly civilised and integrated with the shore as the Mediterranean. It was the same in the twenties, only more so. The competition cult, the almost vicious spirit of rivalry, diffused through every phase and sphere of the fleet's existence, not only failed to bring together, but actually held apart, squadron and squadron, ship and ship, and the individual departments within a ship.

It is clear now – what would have been an extraordinary charge then – that admirals and captains and heads of departments in the Mediterranean fleet shared a practically total ignorance of each other's affairs along with an intense, secretive preoccupation with their own. Temperamentally disinclined to admit an error, Keyes was once heard to confess that he had driven the fleet too hard during his three years at Malta. Everyone beneath him was busy driving his unit hard too, whether it was the First Battle Squadron or H.M.S. *Nonesuch* or the five-man-strong Miscellaneous Division of an insignificant sloop. A non-polo-playing, unaristocratic officer's best bet for advancement was to weld his men – squadron, or ship, or part of a ship – into one of those all-conquering units, the names of which appeared week after week at or near the top of some league table or order of merit in the station orders.

Admiral Keyes was also understood to have said that things might have turned out differently if he had been 'kept informed'. Unit *esprit* developed to the point where offences were concealed, crime hushed up, potentially serious misconduct dealt with surreptitiously, in order that

COMMANDER H. M. DANIEL, D.S.O., R.N.

the unit image might not suffer. Some instances were recorded – and perhaps more were not – of the law having been taken into a comparative junior's own hands, even of matters being settled on the messdeck, that ought to have been aired in a higher court.

The armoured upper deck of a battleship was always a lid on an emotional mixture with a thousand ingredients, bubbling smoothly and hissing predictably most of the time, occasionally erupting under pressure. Eruptions in the Mediterranean fleet, in the circumstances of the mid-twenties, might be expected to have been fewer than normal, but more violent when they occurred. It took little enough to start one: the arrival of a new officer from another station could do it, an officer a little more inquisitive, or sympathetic or conscientious than his predecessor had been.

Dewar and Daniel both agreed, on joining the *Royal Oak*, that she was not altogether the ' happy ship ' everyone seemed to think her: ' outwardly efficient ', her new captain called her, ' but a sort of dead ship, with no enthusiasm and no life '. They put it down to a lack of interest, and communication, between departments and between the ranks. Like the Commander-in-Chief, heads of departments and consequently the Commander and Captain were not being ' kept informed '. The eruptions that broke out about Christmas 1927 were not especially serious but they showed which way the wind had been blowing – apparently for a long time – and they had some significance in the light of subsequent events.

The master-at-arms brought three stokers up before the Commander as defaulters. Superficially, it looked an open-and-shut case: they had, fairly clearly, made a deliberate

assault on a petty officer: an offence against superior authority for which a court martial was the proper answer.
Daniel therefore passed the cases on to Captain Dewar who,
instead of remanding the culprits, asked for an investigation
into the degree of provocation involved.

Provocation? It sounded almost a foreign word in the
Royal Oak. But the Captain had shown some psychic
insight, in being dissatisfied with the preliminary findings.
There had been provocation indeed: the assault, it was at
length determined, had been the last resort of desperate
men, victims of months of private bullying.

Nothing could be done at this stage to save the stokers
but neither Captain nor Commander was convinced that
this was an isolated instance and Dewar particularly wanted
to know: why had they not complained, as the regulations
provided? Looking into this and systematically collecting
evidence in his customary thorough fashion, Daniel dis-
covered that experience on the lower deck taught a man not
to complain. It was dangerous. In what way dangerous?
Everybody knew, said the stokers, that ratings were punished,
or ostracised, or branded sea-lawyers, for laying complaints.
No one in his senses laid a complaint against a senior,
especially if he wanted to get on in the Service.

All this was news to both Dewar and Daniel. Was this
point of view peculiar to the *Royal Oak's* ship's company or
commonly held throughout the fleet – throughout the
Navy? It was impossible to tell. But at the first opportunity – Sunday divisions, when the whole ship's company
was assembled – the Captain got his Commander to read
out the appropriate sections of the Naval Discipline Act and
told the men that as long as he remained in command of the

ship, no one would be punished or victimised for making a grievance known, genuine or not, provided it was done in good faith and the proper Service manner.

The address produced a spate of complaints. For a time it appeared that the *Royal Oak* was positively riddled with hardships and injustices. By far the most serious was one against a commissioned warrant officer, alleging disgraceful misconduct, for which he was to be tried by court martial and dismissed the Service: a satisfactory demonstration of the sincerity with which Dewar had made his promise.

These were hectic days for the *Royal Oak's* senior officers. Far from having 'nothing to do except say what time he wanted a cup of tea', as he had been given to expect, Captain Dewar rarely managed when the ship was in harbour to get home to his wife until a late hour of the night. But, with a new ship to learn about, a new commander to break in, courts martial on his hands and three admirals hovering over him, he found time to launch his personal training course for junior officers, as he had done on the West Indies station; gave it priority, in fact.

He began the new year by introducing the midshipmen to his cherished 'divided tactics' theories of naval warfare. The British Navy, he told them, had only one method of fighting a fleet action and that was in 'single line'. If an enemy did the same a parallel running fight followed, in which tactics played little part: it would be simply an artillery duel, the outcome of which depended on who could stand the pounding longest. "As at present we are pre-eminent (in gunnery efficiency), our policy is sound," said Dewar, "as long as the enemy conforms to similar tactics and desires decisive action." But a long line of ships was not very manoeuvrable and an enemy in divisions (that is, several short lines) could always escape it. ' Single line ' action was popular with admirals because it was easy to lay down definite orders for it, it enabled one man to control the whole fleet, was fairly foolproof from individual stupidity and involved no gunnery complications. " Its dis-advantages," said Dewar, " are the vulnerability of a long line to torpedo attack, its lack of manoeuvring power and the time it takes to deploy." He had always favoured attacks by divisions, where small groups of ships were left free to fight at the range that suited them and could combine in a ' tactical concentration ' – that is to say, could all come together to pour their fire at one part of the enemy fleet. Attack by divisions, he claimed, had never failed on the few occasions it had been tried and no other form of attack had given consistently successful results.

Much of this was above the heads of the midshipmen. They dutifully copied it all down and every Sunday morning the Captain's secretary collected the journals and took them up to the Captain for inspection and signature: something the regulations laid down, something no previous captain had ever done.

Practice followed theory. Dewar told his midshipmen they were going to fight a battle on the tactical table, one side governed by his own ' divided tactics ' system and the other by official *Battle Instructions*. He spent an afternoon demonstrating for them with the model warships, showing how an admiral tried to lead an enemy into such a position that his leading ships came under the concentrated fire of a whole battle-fleet.

Word went round the wardrooms of the First Battle

Squadron that the *Royal Oak* was 'fighting the Battle of Jutland again – showing everybody what Jellicoe ought to have done'. If the Battle of Jutland had to be re-fought, this was the ship to do it: she had been present in that action, next in the line to the fleet flagship, H.M.S. *Iron Duke*.

But a flag-captain's time is never his own and some days, when tactical discussions had to be cut short to allow him to get back on board to attend his admiral, Dewar must have recalled his thoughts on his Staff College disappointment; for the new flag-officer liked entertaining, especially the entertaining of prominent personages, where 'Guard and band' and a flourish of bugles and a formal reception at the gangway was *de rigueur*.

The V.I.P. for Wednesday, 11th January 1928, was the new Governor of Malta, Sir John Philip du Cane, who had just relieved old General Congreve, V.C. He came on board to dine with Admiral Collard, to walk round the upper deck and compliment Daniel on the beautiful enamelling of the after turret (a project the commander had subsidised out of his pay), and to attend a performance at the famous floating cinema.

Next day – the occasion of the wardroom dance, towards the success of which the commander had so strenuously laboured – the Rear-Admiral seemed to have made a special effort to enhance his reputation as a charming and extravagant host by bringing on board the most distinguished guests in Malta: the Commander-in-Chief himself, Admiral Sir Roger Keyes, with Lady Keyes and the rest of the 'House of Keyes' and their current visitors to Admiralty House.

According to Captain Dewar's memories of that evening, no sooner was the Rear-Admiral's dinner party over than he was up on the quarter-deck (where, under fairy lights and a red-and-white-striped ceremonial awning, amid banks of sub-tropical flowers and shrubs, the dance had just begun) irritably enquiring why so many ladies were sitting out without partners and what Commander Daniel, whose instructions about the décor had included no mention of wallflowers, was doing about it.

Daniel, tackled by his captain, protested that the dance had only been in progress for a few minutes, that the programmes were still being filled, that most of the officers were with guests of their own and could not dance with two girls at once – and that everything had been taken care of anyway: he had detailed four or five unattached lieutenants and lieutenant-commanders to look after the wallflowers.

Next moment the Rear-Admiral, ignoring protocol, buttonholed Daniel himself. He was ' very annoyed ' (in the Commander's version of the incident), ordering him to get rid of the marine band and get hold of the ship's jazz band instead. The Commander thought it wise to ' escort his partner to a place of safety ' and then the Admiral took him up to the bandmaster, Mr Barnacle, who had chosen that evening to present some of the latest American airs, sleepy in tempo and unfamiliar to the ears of fox-trotting Mediterranean connoisseurs.

" Come here, you," ordered Collard to the bandmaster (Daniel, shocked as he was, claimed to have remembered every word, *verbatim*). " Come here, you. Stand here. You call yourself a flagship band ? I never heard such a bloody awful noise in my life. Your playing is like a dirge and everybody is complaining. I'll have you sent home and reported to your headquarters."

Dreadfully flustered – it was embarrassing enough for a non-commissioned officer merely to be spoken to by a flag-officer on his flagship's quarter-deck, much less to be the object of an extraordinary outburst like this – Barnacle managed to get out something to the effect that he would do his very best, sir, before Collard turned away and said quite audibly in the silence that preceded the resumption of the music: " I won't have a bugger like that in my ship."

Tactfully to get rid of one orchestra and replace it by another made up of volunteers enticed from their own amusements in their own time, and contriving at the same moment to take care of one's own guests and give scores of others the impression that this small diversion was a routine part of the evening's entertainment – this was typical of the unobtrusive feats of magic a battleship commander regularly had to perform, with a smile, on all kinds of inauspicious occasions. Only a few close bystanders had heard anything untoward; no visitor from shore or from another ship was aware that, behind the screen, a disgusted marine band was handing in its instruments and debating the advisability of ' putting in for a draft' away from the ship. The jazz band assembled without noticeable disgruntlement; Mr Barnacle conducted it apparently without rancour. ' The show , said the midshipman's log, ' appeared to be a complete success '. For a comparative newcomer to the ship, Commander Daniel had done well. At his first big social event in the ship he had managed to throw a neat temporary bridge across a suddenly yawning chasm.

When the evening was discussed and the exact terms of the admiral's remarks disputed, it was the ' my ship ' that infuriated Dewar. The *Royal Oak* was *his* ship, the Rear-

Admiral ' only a passenger '. (Apropos of the relationship, a newspaper was one day to explain: ' In his ship the captain is necessarily a despot. When an admiral arrives with his staff he comes as a self-invited guest . . . supreme over the fleet or the squadron of which the ship forms part, but without authority over its internal affairs. . . . He is a passenger – distinguished, it is true – but still " only a passenger " '.)

Friday, the 13th January, was a big day for Captain Dewar, bigger than usual. First he awoke to a worrying soliloquy about the incredible breach of the peace at the previous evening's dance, that might so disastrously have wrecked it. All forenoon he had distasteful arguments on his mind, as prosecutor in the second of the two courts martial in the ship. (' The evidence was conclusive and the court rose at noon,' was all the midshipman told his diary.) After lunch he hurried to the tactical school, to trot the hobby-horse of ' divided tactics ' once more – and for the last time – round the big table.

It was the last day of the week-long exercise. The battle was working slowly to a climax. Collard was there – he had readily agreed, before it began, to preside and umpire. Admirals Keyes and Kelly were there too, much to the gratification of spectators who attached importance to being seen about, yet who had only gone along to the educational building for want of something better to do. This was a big day for the centre, too: no fuller house had ever been seen within the memory of those present, except at fleet exercise ' wash-ups '. Oblivious of the crowd, and the unexpected presence of the Commander-in-Chief and the

Second-in-Command of the Mediterranean fleet – or perhaps for their benefit – Dewar had pressed ahead with the indoctrination of his officers.

Priceless opportunities, he had said earlier, were sacrificed to the fetish of keeping in line, when admirals manoeuvred fleets in battle. Every action followed the same pattern, there were no surprises. First, the fleets advanced in column; second, they turned at right-angles into line ahead; third, they fought a running action on parallel courses. This was what he meant when he spoke of ' rigid line ' tactics.

The problem set for solution on the table this week was: how could a battle-fleet using ' divided tactics ', operating by divisions widely separated from each other, achieve concentration and victory over one that operated conventionally? This Friday afternoon the situation, after four days of skirmishing and jockeying for advantage, was poised to vindicate or condemn his theories. One fleet had acted throughout under the full control of its ' Commander-in-Chief ', the other (under Dewar) had been given liberty of action under its individual squadron ' admirals ' and flotilla ' captains '.

Some realism was lacking, and Dewar at a disadvantage, because the ' enemy ' knew he was demonstrating divided tactics and therefore had no chance of gaining a sharp advantage by some surprise movement. The engagement, which had looked full of promise when the day began, ended after all in stalemate. Or had it? Both sides claimed a victory, or what would have been a victory had not time run out; both claimed they ended the battle in a winning position. But it was getting late, and Rear-Admiral Collard reserved judgment until the following day.

All the participants and spectators were back at nine o'clock on Saturday morning, either to hear the Flag-Officer's summing up or in expectation of another visit from Admirals Keyes and Kelly. They were satisfied on both counts. The Commander-in-Chief and his second-in-command arrived with a sprinkling of their staffs. And, after the somewhat dull, inconclusive moves and counter-moves of the previous part of the war game, all found Collard brilliant entertainment.

Stocky and erect at the head of the table the Rear-Admiral, in his deep, hoarse voice and a few unminced words, delivered an attack that was evidently meant to dispose of divided tactics once and for all. He roundly derided his flag-captain's handling of the model fleet. In spite of the time he had given himself, he said, for the un-hurried consideration of every move, Dewar had failed to achieve in four clear days anything resembling the tactical concentration he was after. What would happen in time of war, when decisions were split-second ones and the atmosphere very different from that around the tactical table, could be left to the imagination. To put it mildly, this was a system bound to lead to fatal blunders. There was in any case nothing new about it. These theories had all been propounded and thrashed out and discarded years ago.

Captain Dewar politely disagreed. "I must remind Admiral Collard that when my time ran out the battle-cruisers *were* concentrating. They were fast closing the enemy's rear and had opened fire on his destroyer screen."

"You secured no tactical advantage," rasped Collard. "That last move of yours would have allowed the enemy equally to gain a partial concentration on your own main fleet. I am talking abour real-life situations, not tactical board ones. A good many contingencies occur in live actions that cannot be provided for on the tactical table. You can't lay smoke-screens, for a start – which would undoubtedly have been done if this engagement had taken place at sea."

Dewar was ready to contest this viewpoint in his usual outspoken fashion, but the Flag-Officer was in no mood for an argument and abruptly closed the session. The midshipmen returned on board with their eyes opened: they were yet to learn that war games frequently end in acrimonious dispute and claims of victory on both sides, and are to that extent just like the real thing. Some were seeing a captain reproved by an admiral for the first time – and in the presence of his officers. Was it conceivable, the writer of the log asked himself, that even an admiral might—? No, that was too far-fetched.

" The old boy fairly went for the Captain this morning," the midshipman told a messmate whom duty had kept on board. But in his journal he only wrote:

' We had a very good hockey match against the *Queen Elizabeth*, which we won 3–2.'

CHAPTER VII

After the Ball

Just how serious, in retrospect, was the fracas at the dance?
One of the *Royal Oak's* married officers went ashore to his
furnished flat, on the day the war game ended, to report that
the ship was seething with discontent. His wife could not
understand why. She had been one of the lucky ones, one
of the ladies who had been standing close enough to the
band and the Admiral to hear every word of the outburst.
Until the ' snake pit ' had engorged the titbit of gossip, she
was a centre of attraction. She had been invited to tea on
' Snob street ' (Pietà hill, where the more fashionable naval
families lived) more times in one day than in all the months
she had lived in Valletta. Far from being insulted, she told
her husband, the feminine side of the fleet was ' hugely
delighted '. Anyhow, the music *had* been rather dismal.
Who better to complain about it than racy little Sammy
Collard? Was not that what admirals were for, to fly off
the handle and keep people on their toes?

She spoke for practically the whole of the civilian population. The new rear-admiral in the Battle Squadron was a
bright, uninhibited flag-officer, a change from his pre-
decessors. Was it correct that he liked a party above everything? He had certainly gone to one about Christmas time
in fancy dress: in a pram, sucking a dummy, pushed by his
flag-lieutenant in nurse's cap and apron. Odd behaviour,

for an *admiral*. Yes, but had anyone heard how he started a mutiny at Portsmouth, back in 1906?

The wardrooms and officers' clubs took it calmly enough. Whatever had happened, it had not sunk the ship. It was the *Royal Oak's* affair in any case, no business of anyone else, dismissible in some such exchange as:

" Sammy Collard overdid it a bit the other night."

" Sammy? Oh, Sammy's a character. Doesn't surprise me a bit to hear that."

Nor could the *Royal Oak* herself fairly be said to have ' seethed with discontent '. The midshipman marked the occasion with an entry: ' There was a small dance on the quarter-deck . . . fortunately the night was fine and the show appeared to be a complete success. The ship's company band assisted with the music '. One officer who saw the evening through from start to finish knew nothing about the outburst until, months later, after he had left the ship, someone who had *not* been present told him. On the lower deck, at least on the sailors' part of it, a supposed insult to a mere marine – and a marine bandsman, at that – was no matter for indignation. The fleet boxing finals, held the same night, rated much more passionate debate. Who cared what an admiral said? He was on his flagship's quarter-deck, he could say what he liked. A good deal of salt water was to flow under the *Royal Oak's* keel before that hackneyed bit of Service backchat emerged, applicable equally to cooks and coxswains and captains: "Who called the bandmaster a bugger?" – "You mean, who called the bugger a bandmaster?"

But one or two of the *Royal Oak's* senior officers felt there was a mess to be swept up – and perhaps someone's nose to be rubbed in it. Captain and Commander were especially concerned. At the end of the dance Admiral Collard had renewed his threat about getting rid of the bandmaster and had got so angry and noisy and red-faced with them that they had feared it might almost have developed into a scuffle.

The day after the dance, Commander Daniel sent for Mr Barnacle and opened a long interview by telling him 'not to take it too seriously'. If he were not disposed to take it seriously then, he was taking it seriously enough by the time he left the Commander's cabin. Later he went to see the Chaplain and came up with a request to leave the Service, offering to forfeit all his pension rights. Later still two members of the marine band put in their applications to leave the ship. And after that the Major of Marines himself, Major Claude Attwood, appeared, very stiff and correct, to register a formal protest about the 'insult to his corps'.

Up at the tactical school the war game was petering out and Rear-Admiral Collard preparing to deal his flag-captain some damaging and not-easily-to-be-forgiven blows to prestige. When the party returned on board, Daniel, on his way to see the Captain, was told that the Admiral wanted to see *him*. He found both Collard and Dewar in the cabin.

"Look here, Commander," said the Admiral without preliminaries, "the Chaplain has just been here and accused me of calling the bandmaster a bugger. You were with me, now, and know I did nothing of the sort." Daniel thought for a moment and answered carefully:

"If you ask me whether you called the bandmaster that

name, I am bound to answer ' No '. But if you ask me, sir, whether you referred to him by that name in my hearing, then my answer must be ' Yes '. And nothing will alter my recollection of the incident."

At this (it is still Daniel's version of the history) Admiral Collard grew hot-tempered again and shouted in his raucous, overbearing voice that it was a lie, he had said no such thing. Daniel took the wind out of his sails by saying politely to the Captain, " I have the Major outside, sir. He wishes to protest to the Admiral on behalf of the corps." Collard dropped his blustering attitude and asked, almost diffidently, what was to be done?

Dewar shrugged the question off on his second-in-command. It would be best, said Daniel, to leave everything to him. The ' unwarranted attack on a rating who could not answer back at an important social occasion ' had caused ' not only a great deal of discontent on the lower deck but also intense disgust and indignation among the officers '. He asked for *carte blanche* to try and get the thing smoothed over. As executive officer of the ship (though a newcomer), responsible for its discipline and welfare, he had a good idea how to proceed, what kind of explanation officers and men would respond to. He would, of course, keep the Admiral informed.

The Captain thought this a most sensible suggestion. The Admiral agreed. Pressed further (the subsequent courts had Daniel's word for it) he agreed that an apology might be conveyed to Bandmaster Barnacle for a start.

The Flag-Officer's account of this meeting, which differed from Dewar's and Daniel's, was not disclosed until he came to be examined as a witness in court. Neither then nor later did Collard speak of his predicament, to wife ashore in Malta, or to staff officer or flag-lieutenant or fellow admiral. When, weeks afterwards, the journalists were gathering with offers to ' help him lay his case before the public ', and suggestions that silence condemned, that reluctance to talk was halfway to being an admission of guilt, Collard still kept his own counsel. Such remarks as he made to reporters, off the rough edge of his tongue, were unquotable. Collard and Dewar were approximately of an age but by temperament and outlook they belonged to different worlds – one a new-look type of naval officer, the other among the last of a vintage brand. In no respect was the difference more marked than in their individual attitudes to publicity.

On Sunday, the 15th January, spring came to Malta. The gloomy skies that had hung over the island passed northwards and the place turned on the kind of warm, bright day that only Malta in January can. The ramparts were suddenly alive with mauve creeper and dotted with clumps of rock flowers, and the scent of narcissi drifted in waves over Valletta. Down in Grand Harbour where, at the yard-arms of warships, red-white-and-blue church pendants hung limp in the morning air, a flag-officer's barge sped across the roadstead and martial airs floated back from the *Royal Oak's* ' Guard and band ' on the quarter-deck as Rear-Admiral and Mrs Collard, the Flag-Lieutenant and one or two guests, went aboard for divine service. Captain Dewar was ashore that forenoon, but the Commander was there to receive the party with his usual attentive courtesy, supported by the Major of Marines (in charge of the guard today) and the Chaplain, Harry Goulding.

When church was over, Commander Daniel sent a

message to the day cabin asking if the Admiral would join the officers for a pre-lunch cocktail in the wardroom. Collard would, with pleasure. He stayed for twenty minutes, accepted the ' other half ' and diffused much good fellowship. The Commander followed him out when he left, to mention that his apology to Mr Barnacle had ' made a considerable impression on the ship's company '. The marines were satisfied, the band would not be putting in to leave the ship after all. " Thank you," beamed Collard, full of bonhomie this morning, " thank you for getting me out of a damned nasty hole." Such, at least, was the way Daniel told it. He went back to the wardroom, he afterwards claimed, and said to all the officers: " It's all right. The Admiral has taken our salt. The incident is closed." One or two wondered what incident he was talking about.

Early next week the Rear-Admiral received a summons from his immediate superior, Vice-Admiral John D. Kelly. They stood on the *Warspite's* sternwalk together and talked.

The dance gossip had not reached the Vice-Admiral's ears – not yet, or not officially. It was the war game he wanted to discuss.

" Sammy, the Commander-in-Chief is a little perturbed. He says there seems to be some friction between yourself and Dewar. He particularly noticed it on Saturday; thought you were a little hard on him and that he plainly resented it. Have you quarrelled? Is he being difficult? "

It was a happy chance for the junior flag-officer to say yes, things were difficult, insignificant trifles had assumed serious proportions; that, from the day he hoisted his flag, he had not found Dewar easy to put up with; that his flag-captain

and the ship's commander were of a type he did not trust –
brooding, sensitive, *clever* fellows – and of a mentality whose
devious ways he could not fathom. He thought for a while,
then replied.

There *had* been a small difficulty, he admitted, but a minor
one, soon resolved. It was only a matter of shaking down
together. He felt quite confident of dealing with any
situation that might arise. He had a high opinion of his
flag-captain, and of his flagship. He wished for no change
of either.

Thus, with an answer that was the only possible one from
an officer brought up in Collard's school, with its old-
fashioned code of loyalty to colleagues above and below, the
opportunity passed. And the weeks rolled by.

Dewar had discontinued his tactical exercises and War
College lecture programme. The fleet was leaving Malta
in any case, for the spring cruise to Greek waters. The
descriptions and the diagrams in the midshipmen's journals
now concerned the *Royal Oak's* latest keep-fit craze: obstacle
races for the whole ship's company, involving a wall-
climbing expedition over the four turrets, every afternoon
during the passage to Syra; invented by Commander
Daniel.

But Sir Roger Keyes seemed to have caught something
of Dewar's obsession with experimental manoeuvres. On
the way back to Malta in February he announced some
daring exercises for the Battle Squadron. A new plan for
carrying out a ' blue turn ' in the middle of a ' white turn ',
invented by the French, was among them – in plain language,
a method of turning a line of ships simultaneously to a new

course while there was a kink in the line. It was a manoeuvre prohibited in the regulations because of the danger of collision.

For almost a month the *Royal Oak* was immobilised in Grand Harbour, carrying out a self-refit alongside Parlatorio wharf. ' A great deal of entertaining went on ', wrote the midshipman. ' On Wednesday the wardroom gave a dance, on Thursday the marine officers and wives were at home to the wives of the ship's company, on Friday the " Oak Leaves " gave a concert, on Saturday the ship's company gave a dance on board to which a large number of people came off from shore and everything went very successfully.'

Most of the crew were busy painting or boiler-cleaning apart from this, and the gunroom could find no team to play hockey with except the band, under the obliging but ludicrous captaincy of Mr Barnacle. The rest of the Mediterranean fleet was at sea for most of February, and when two old friends and rivals came in – the *Resolution* and the *Ramillies*, fresh from refits in England – they went straight out again to join the flag. It was the carnival season ashore, the time of year when the influx of British visitors reached a peak. The *Royal Oak's* officers, dizzy with the effort of keeping up with the accelerated social round, found the stiff programme of post-refit trials relaxing by comparison – or would have done, had not everything gone wrong from the moment the ship rounded St Elmo's point.

Ships, like men and racehorses, have their off-days, sometimes a whole series of them one after another. H.M.S. *Royal Oak* struck her bad patch on the 3rd March, when a high-angle gun jammed during a shoot and ordnance officers had to be signalled for. She anchored for the night in Mellieha bay and, on weighing in the early hours for a star-shell practice, her cable officer, O'Donnell, could not get the anchor up. The capstan-engine had failed and the cable had to be back-achingly recovered 'handraulically'. When at last he got the 15-inch broadsides away (O'Donnell was gunnery officer as well), they were unbelievably bad; the 6-inch were worse; and to cap thirty-six hours of misery, all the director training circuits failed at a critical moment.

Only those most intimately concerned with the day-to-day activities of the three senior officers could suspect tension between them. The Flag-Lieutenant may have noticed it; so may the chief yeoman and the Captain's chief steward, the Navigating Commander and the Admiral's coxswain; few others. Superficially, relations were cordial. Daniel, indeed, gripped by 'promotionitis', of which the symptoms are a restless urge to interfere with everyone else's job, made himself almost embarrassingly pleasant to the Admiral and was clearly on the best of terms with the Captain. Dewar, by what seemed mere coincidence, appeared to see little of his flag-officer on board, except to attend him when arriving or leaving. But they went for a walk together while the *Royal Oak* lay in Dragamesti Bay. Traditionally the Flag-Captain messed with the Admiral and the rest of his staff, but the ship was mostly at Malta these days and they both had wives ashore. Collard – was Collard: sharp of eye, raucous of voice, quick and racy of speech, a little Napoleonic figure limping up and down the *Royal Oak's* bridge or quarter-deck, outspoken and dictatorial and pompous, so confident a squadron admiral and so much in command that Sir Roger Keyes had privately told him he would be allowed to take the fleet to sea, when it left Malta for the annual combined exercises in mid-March: a remarkable sign of favour to one so junior and so recently arrived on the station.

Low cloud and a heavy south-easterly swell with a cross-wind made it too rough for towing targets on Monday, the 5th March, and the rest of the ship's two-day gunnery programme was cancelled. But on the forecastle the sweating and straining continued. The capstan-engine was working again, but now an anchor had jammed in the hawse-pipe and locked the cable-holder, so the watch on deck was up late once again, on a wet and windswept fore-castle, hauling off the cable and changing it end for end with Weston's purchases. The *Royal Oak* returned to harbour. The spray leaped high on the low cliffs around the island, the breakwater was awash and St Elmo's light shedding an unusually lurid glare on a wild-looking sea. Inside Grand Harbour, where the wind came down fiercely off the heights, the fleet had hoisted its boats and frapped its awnings and all the dghaisas had gone away into the backwaters for shelter.

Outside it was choppy and unpleasant even for a ship of the *Royal Oak's* size. There was mist about, and darkness and heavy weather in the Malta channel when the Captain shaped up for his anchorage off the breakwater.

Originally the ship had been due to return at eleven p.m., and the Flag-Lieutenant, Burghard, had ordered the barge to come out and meet her at that time, to take the Admiral ashore. (He was to preside at a court martial in the *Valiant* next day.) But now the Commander was having the in-formation broadcast that ' Ship is expected to anchor about eight-forty-five' and the Admiral was revising his plans. 'Flags' gave the Commander his instructions: the barge's routine was advanced two hours; the Admiral wanted a gangway rigged on the quarter-deck, but not lowered until he saw what the weather was like in the anchorage; in case it was too rough for boats to come alongside, he required a boat-rope and Jacob's ladder on the boom, and yardarm illumination overhead. (One of Collard's less endearing habits, thought Daniel while 'hoisting in' the orders, was his fondness for giving minute instructions, as though for the benefit of someone of strictly limited intelligence. Today they implied that the Admiral could trust no one else on board to take normal seamanlike precautions for disembarking in a swell.)

What had not been specified (unless it had been lost in transmission) was which side of the quarter-deck the Admiral intended to disembark from. Daniel assumed he had no particular preference. Calculating the probable lie of the ship after she swung to her anchor he decided that starboard would be the safer and he gave instructions to that effect to Lieutenant Phillips, whom he had put in charge of the preparations. He himself returned to the forecastle to work with O'Donnell on the stubborn cable-holder.

Nothing would shift it. The capstan-engine had seized again, was going to take hours to repair. Daniel informed the Captain that only the starboard anchor was available for letting go that night, and he stayed on the forecastle with the cable party to make sure nothing else went wrong.

At nine o'clock the ship, her engines stopped, was creeping towards her appointed berth for the night. At three minutes past, the signal to let go the anchor flashed down from the bridge, the cable ran out satisfactorily, and the Commander walked aft for the next item on the programme: seeing the Admiral ashore. On the way a messenger intercepted him. From Lieutenant Phillips, would he come at once, please, because the Admiral was asking for him.

On the quarter-deck, swept by the pendulum beam of a yardarm group oscillating in the wind, clustered an unhappy knot of junior officers and ratings. Phillips just had time to whisper that he had got the wrong gangway out and the Admiral was livid before Collard stumped down on them. He was ' indeed furious ', the Commander later recalled; ' demanding to know why the port ladder was not ready in spite of orders given by the Flag-Lieutenant two hours earlier '. Daniel, foreseeing another outrageous exhibition in the presence of juniors, had already made up his mind not to argue or exacerbate the feelings of one who, he was beginning to think, might not be altogether responsible for his actions.

" . . . And see to it yourself," roared Collard, concluding his tirade.

" Aye, aye, sir."

The Commander saluted. Peace was going to be bought cheaply enough, at the price of a new gangway – for it was obviously asking for trouble to put it over the port side. As for a wrecked barge and perhaps drowned men, that was the Admiral's problem. Then it dawned on him that the Admiral wanted to leave the ship at once, before she had swung to her anchored position. The barge was already lying off, waiting to come alongside, rolling heavily to judge by the way her navigation lights and searchlight dipped. In eight minutes the port gangway was down, as fast as ever it had been turned out. And the barge came easily alongside in calm water. There had been method enough in Collard's apparent madness. Until the ship bore down and took up her position head to wind, this was the lee side.

' Flags ' was in the boat. The Admiral followed him, in a flurry of salutes from gangway staff, midshipman of the watch, officer of the watch, duty lieutenant-commander, Commander – and Captain. Dewar had hurried off the bridge as soon as he could; just in time to catch a hailstorm of abuse.

' No ladder, nothing . . . not fit to be a flagship . . . treated worse than an ordinary seaman . . . fed up with the ship ' – one or two people heard the phrases, blown back on the wind. The last thing they heard, as he went over the side, was Collard's hoarse: " I should damn well think so. And get the Commander's reasons in writing." A startled lieutenant told his confrères in the wardroom that the Admiral had " just gone for Henry like a pickpocket, most undignified behaviour you ever saw." A midshipman on the quarter-deck (at the subsequent court martial he was allowed to remain anonymous) testified to Admiral Collard's ' loud voice and heated manner '. In the seamen petty officers' mess it was disclosed, more graphically, that the ' scrambled eggs ' (oak leaves) on the flag-officer's cap were ' sizzling '.

Scenes like this, so wounding to the self-respect of a sensitive officer when they take place in his subordinates' hearing, are infrequent but by no means unknown in the Royal Navy. Dewar himself told of a captain who ordered the signalman to ' bring him a bucket, the commander made him sick '. But Daniel was profoundly affected. That evening in the Captain's cabin he poured out the full tale of the ' great commotion ' at the gangway. The Admiral was tactless, unfair, domineering and the rudest man he had ever met. He had his knife in the ship, nothing would please him, he was destroying morale faster than Daniel could build it up. . . . For the insults to himself, said Daniel, speaking rapidly and nervously, he cared nothing; it was the effect on the ship that worried him. Things simply could not go on any longer, he was throwing his hand in.

Contemporaries said later that a superior less emotionally involved already than Dewar was, or one who took himself less seriously, or one who had not reached the same conclusion, that changes must be made – almost any battleship captain in the Service, except Kenneth Dewar at that moment, would have soothed his commander with a glass of port and put off a detailed discussion until tempers were cooler all round; would have helped with the concoction of the ' reasons in writing ' (a formal explanation of failure to perform some duty) in a dignified and unprovocative strain. But Daniel left the Captain's cabin that night knowing exactly where Dewar's sympathies lay. If he did not, he would have learned anyway at about five o'clock the following afternoon.

Collard had been pondering too, and seeing eye to eye with Flag-Captain and Commander in at least one respect: that this state of affairs could not continue. Was the flagship triumvirate to be dissolved, or forced into the proper mould ? Was he to stick it out, make Dewar and Daniel toe the line, or shift his flag to a more amenable ship ? (The thought that he might have got rid of one or both of them he char-

acteristically dismissed: it would have harmed their careers.)
Whatever he made up his mind to do, events moved too
quickly for him to do it.

The smart blue-and-white-painted barge with its neat
badges and rear-admiral's flag (a St George's cross with two
red discs) throbbed out beyond the breakwater and slid
alongside the *Royal Oak*. On sighting her, the bo'sun's mate
detailed to keep a lookout had put the customary routine
into operation, informing the petty officer quartermaster,
who told the officer of the watch. The officer of the watch
had sent a message to the duty lieutenant-commander and
to the Commander, who notified the Captain. And they
all stood at the gangway and at the salute while the bugle
sounded the ' Still ' and a chorus of pipes shrilled twice –
once as the barge came alongside, once as the Flag-Officer
came up the gangway.

Collard reached the top and stood on the platform and
glared round him. " Men: get down that ladder and attend
to the boat-ropes," he called to some of the duty hands
waiting to hoist the boat. Then he turned and limped off
to his quarters without a glance or a word, or a sign of
acknowledgment of the presence of his flag-captain and
the officers.

Pale with anger, Dewar disappeared down his own
hatchway. When, next day, the Commander brought in
his ' reasons in writing ', the Captain was composing a
formal complaint about the ' studied insult ', as he called it,
just offered him in the presence of his officers and ship's
company.

He broke off to read through the lengthy *apologia* in

which his second-in-command, to explain his part in the
'gangway commotion' had found it necessary to go back
to the dance incident of January. There was also an
important tailpiece:

'This concludes my report on the event, but I consider it
my duty to point out what serious harm is done by such
incidents. On the last occasion great pains were necessary
to restore the respect of the Admiral in the public opinion
of the wardroom and the lower deck and I feel confident
this has been achieved. This occurrence, together with and
emphasised by the insult before nearly a hundred officers
and men at 1745 yesterday has had a very serious effect on
morale and discipline. Among the wardroom officers,
those who had the mortifying experience of witnessing these
scenes are inflamed with indignation and all officers are
deeply resentful of the humiliation to which they see their
Captain and ship have been subjected. I myself was not
personally affronted by any words used by the Admiral to
me, my sole reason for representing this state of affairs is
that I consider the morale of the ship the special care of the
Commander, and I should be guilty of neglect and cowardice
if I shrank from asking that a protest should be made in the
most generous but uncompromising way possible at your
discretion. Apologies would serve no useful purpose, but
assurance is urgently necessary that discipline, which must
depend on respect for rank, will not be undermined in this
way.

'Moreover I wish to draw your attention to the inevitable
apprehensions which prevail concerning the forthcoming
Admiral's inspection. The ship is discouraged. My recent
appeal to look forward to the inspection, thereby making it

serve a useful purpose for the efficiency of the Service, has been reversed by anticipation of vindictive fault-finding.'

So ended Commander Daniel's ' reasons in writing ', the explanation of his failure to meet the Admiral's wishes in the matter of a gangway. They were addressed to his captain, to whom he was responsible for the internal work of the ship. The question was, where did Dewar go from here? ' Reasons in writing ' normally finished off an incident, it was the usual way of dealing with cause for complaint; but this letter looked more like the start of one. This, Dewar decided, after studying it again carefully, could not just be put away in the confidential file and destroyed at the end of the commission.

He had to take the ship to sea again that day for more gunnery trials, and in the evening, on anchoring, he sent for the Commander and asked if he would not prefer to delete the last paragraphs of his letter, or at least modify the tone of them. To him it seemed they might have been more tactfully worded.

But Daniel thought it a rather good letter and stuck by every word of it. Dewar then formally accepted it, and got to work on one of his own, for transmission to Vice-Admiral Kelly, his ' administrative authority ' (although, like all submissions to higher authority, it would be passed through his immediate superior, Rear-Admiral Collard). It was a letter of the type he must often have been tempted to write, a round such as he must often have wanted to loose off in paper battles on the campaign grounds of Admiralty and gunnery school.

' Sir ', it began, ' I am extremely loth to make a complaint against a senior officer, Rear-Admiral Bernard St George

Collard, but I have no alternative as his behaviour is calculated to undermine not only my position but also the general discipline of the ship which I have the honour to command. . . . The incidents complained of are described below.

'At an evening dance given aboard the *Royal Oak* on 12th January, Rear-Admiral Collard threatened me in the hearing of several guests that if I did not make the Commander do his duty in introducing people to each other he would make me rue it. . . . Later in the evening the Rear-Admiral sent for the executive officer, Commander Daniel, and told him to clear the marine band off the quarter-deck. He then walked to where the band was playing and, having called the bandmaster, proceeded to abuse him. . . . Despite the unreasonableness of the Rear-Admiral's demands, his wishes were instantly carried out . . . it required a great deal of persuasion on the Commander's part to prevail upon (the volunteer jazz band) to play and so avoid a disgraceful fiasco.

'While the guests were leaving the ship at the end of the dance the Rear-Admiral addressed me at the gangway to the effect that he would not have the bandmaster in the flagship and that he was to be sent home without delay. When I respectfully protested the Rear-Admiral became excited and only with difficulty was another scene avoided.'

Dewar's letter went on to describe in meticulous detail how the Admiral had subsequently climbed down from a despotic perch under pressure from himself and the Commander, Chaplain and others, and had given Daniel authority to apologise in his name to those individuals insulted. ' I

directed ', said the last paragraph of this part of the report,
' that, whilst endeavouring to preserve the dignity of the
Rear-Admiral the interests of the Service must come first
. . . I made it clear that grievous harm had been done and
that in future the ship would be my first consideration '.

The second half of the letter explained how a truce had
been broken – by the ' gangway commotion ' of 5th March:

' Before anchoring I had got a good swing on the ship
with the engines in order to bring her quickly head to wind,
but before the cable had run out I received a message that
the Admiral wanted me on the quarter-deck. I at once went
aft and found him in a very excited state about five yards
abaft the davit of the port ladder, where a number of men
were working. He at once commenced a threatening and
aggressive tirade, the main points of which were – (a) he
could not get a single order obeyed in the bloody ship – no
ladder, no nothing; (b) he was treated worse than a midshipman; (c) he would not stay in this rotten ship and would
ask to have his flag shifted.

' The trouble was that the Rear-Admiral wanted to use
the port accommodation ladder while the ship was still
swinging fast. . . . In regard to the statement that orders
were never obeyed, I submit that on this occasion they were
obeyed literally and in the spirit. On demand, the Rear-
Admiral failed to show any occasion on which orders had
not been obeyed.'

The report continued with the story of the ' unacknow-
ledged salute ' incident of the following day and ended:
' (Rear-Admiral Collard's) general attitude and demeanour
had every appearance of a *studied insult* to me in the presence
of a large number of officers and men.'

Dewar's letter outran his second-in-command's reasons in writing (lengthy as they had been) by several hundred words. His secretary, Paymaster Lieutenant-Commander Crichton, sat late into the night behind a locked cabin door typing out the numerous copies of both that Mediterranean fleet regulations insisted on, whenever submissions from juniors to seniors were made.

Dewar was going to pass both letters on, the one to support the other. Captain and Commander would stand or fall together.

CHAPTER VIII

Fat in the Fire

THE shoot, Lieutenant-Commander O'Donnell in the spotting top told his second gunnery officer, was a shambles. "H.M.S. 'Oodoo, this is," a control-party rating was heard to mutter as he climbed up through the manhole from the forty-foot straight and wedged himself into his small bucket seat. Far below, the *Royal Oak's* low grey bows gently dipped and recovered and the blue Mediterranean creamed languidly past, frothing white over the forecastle as the ship started to swing into her 180-degree turn to make another run.

"' X ' turret closed up, cleared away, securing chains off, bore clear, all circuits tested and correct," rattled out of the headphones. The gunnery officer nodded. "Stand by." Outside his small steel tower a red flag ascended from the 'dip' to the 'close up'. "Ready to open fire."

On the beam, almost over the horizon, two tugs towed what looked like floating cricket sight-screens, in line ahead. These were the targets. "For exercise, for exercise, for exercise. Alarm starboard. Enemy in sight bearing green five-oh—"

"' A ' turret on—"

"' B ' turret on—"

"' Y ' turret won't bear," came a cry from the aftermost turret. Until the ship steadied on her new course, the target was outside its arc of fire. "Salvoes!"

Little blue lights flickered on in the spotting top, telling O'Donnell as each circuit was complete. The interceptors were closed, five hundred men and fifty expensive instruments had filled in the complex pattern of calculation and it needed only a finger on a button to release several tons of high explosive. " Shoot."

For the next ten minutes, while the battleship steamed at high speed on a parallel course with the target-towing vessel on the horizon, her guns thundered out a succession of salvoes and broadsides. Each time, at the crash and jerk of the explosion, the ship seemed momentarily to rein up in her course, quiver and move forward again. Each time the dust and soot, shaken loose with the shock, descended from invisible crannies in the spotting top deckhead; and each time a dirty, brown-black cloud of chemical-smelling smoke billowed out and drifted astern.

" Check, check, check . . . all guns half-cock . . . train on lookout bearing— " Now the *Royal Oak* was slow ahead, closing the targets, and from conning tower and compass platform, director and armoured tower and spotting top, binoculars were intently trained for evidence of that accuracy of controlled shooting that made or marred the reputation of captain and gunnery officer and ship. And silence, except for the senile crackle and hiss of the communication line, fell on the turrets and control positions.

" Secure."

That meant fall out from action stations. The run was over. For once, everything had gone right, not only had practically every broadside straddled the target (the Captain called up the voice-pipe) but some shells had holed it and now they had parted the tow-line. The *Royal Oak*, followed by *Ramillies* and *Resolution*, who had not done so well, was returning to harbour.

The three ships were acting as one division today, under Rear-Admiral Collard's command. It was a two-hour run back to Malta from the exercise area; getting dark, and a confusion of lights shifted and twinkled on the surface of Grand Harbour. Under the old walls of the citadel it was flat calm, and droves of dghaisas, worse than on regatta day, scurried across the big ships' bows as they ploughed towards their berths.

Dewar had turned in the congested space and now had the *Royal Oak* aimed at the buoy with her engines stopped, gliding up to it . . . when Admiral Collard, standing with his Flag-Lieutenant and Staff Officer on the lower bridge, asked, " Why is this ship going to the wrong buoy? She ought to go to Number 12." Hasty enquiry from Captain Dewar produced the information that the berths had been changed during the previous night by the harbour authority, and that *Royal Oak's* buoy was now Number 13. There had been a signal about it.

The *Ramillies* was closely following and, with *Royal Oak* now swung across the harbour, an alarming situation had developed: it was not improbable that the Flag-Officer – under the eyes of the Commander-in-Chief, as he was only too keenly aware – would distinguish himself in the next few minutes by procuring a magnificent pile-up of battleships. With difficulty the *Ramillies* was stopped in time, and the *Resolution* astern of her. The tension, as these ships manoeuvred through a narrow space between the *Royal Oak* and the aircraft carrier *Eagle* at the adjoining buoys to get to their berths in the inner harbour, left even Collard breathless.

All night and all next day the battleships, and every other ship at Malta, had store-boats and lighters clustering round them, provisioning and ammunitioning and taking on torpedoes and 'topping-up' in every direction. The following afternoon the fleet was due to sail for the combined exercises with the Atlantic fleet, the great annual spring 'war' – the last, incidentally, that Sir Roger Keyes would conduct, for in three months or less he was due to leave his command.

The *Royal Oak's* midshipman kept two whole pages blank in his journal for a description of the mass departure on the Saturday afternoon. In the end, he made only one entry: 'a.m. Completed with ammunition'. The events of the following day were just as disappointingly glossed over:

'11th March 1928. At Malta. The *Berwick* called on passage to China. The Admiral, Captain and Commander left the ship.'

Whatever advice a sympathiser, had there been one at hand, might have given Dewar and Daniel about the wisdom of writing or forwarding their letters, no one could deny it was done at the most inconvenient time imaginable. The 'gangway commotion' arose on the night of Monday, 5th March, and the 'studied insult' was offered the next afternoon. Daniel gave the Captain his 'reasons in writing' on Wednesday and Dewar passed the letter on, along with his own, on Thursday. Rear-Admiral Collard kept them for twenty-four hours and Vice-Admiral Kelly got them in the afternoon of Friday, by special delivery.

Receiving intelligence of a kind that in the best of circumstances gives senior officers ulcers, he must have had among his first reactions the thought: why did it have to happen now? For the ships of the Battle Squadron were at full stretch, getting in supplies and raising steam and preparing to sail, in exactly one day from now, for the most elaborate set of manoeuvres the Malta command had ever devised; with a timetable more sacred than ever, because all the arrangements were dovetailed in with an equally complex series prepared for the Atlantic fleet, both having for their *grande finale* a mock battle off the island of Alboran and a ceremonial entry in company into Gibraltar bay.

The complainants perhaps considered the crisis beautifully timed: it meant the showdown must come quickly and be done with. Kelly, preoccupied with the question of leading his squadron to sea next day, would send for Collard, swiftly and unambiguously reprimand him, warn him about his future conduct and, in the not-too-distant future, find a convincing reason for getting him to shift his flag; and the *Royal Oak* would become a private ship again, the way Dewar had always wanted her.

So the Captain imagined. He himself was prepared for a rebuke of the ' faults on both sides ' order. Sooner or later, he expected, the row would come to the ears of the Commander-in-Chief – a useful information service operated among the staff and there were not many gossip items or hints of strained relationships, professional or marital, that went unreported to the ' House of Keyes '. It would be worth it, to get the affair cleared up.

He miscalculated. The promoter of ' independent thought ' should have known better, he who had diagnosed stultification and tactical paralysis in the Navy's higher ranks for years – ailments contracted from exposure to the staff system. Squadron admirals were only the more prominent performers in the circus that moved under the ring-mastery of naval headquarters in Malta. When even the daily magazine temperatures had to be reported to the fleet flagship, when the simplest request from a junior rating to exchange ships with a friend had to be referred to the Commander-in-Chief for approval – was it likely that a tricky business like this, involving a rear-admiral, a captain and a commander, would be voluntarily shouldered by Joe Kelly? Dynamite: straight to C.-in-C.: he was too old a hand, too old a friend of Sir Roger Keyes, for anything else.

" . . . The ship is under sailing orders." It was being piped, along with details of restricted leave to the watch ashore in H.M.S. *Warspite*, as Admiral Kelly went through the letters again. Another Staveley-Martyn affair, bad blood in the flagship. Arbitrating between two such awkward customers as Collard and Dewar, opinionated and different as chalk from cheese, would be a thankless job. Daniel he did not know much about, but the fellow sounded a rare sea-lawyer. Wrote plays, did he? Joe Kelly might have known.

' Expected time of Departure ' was six hours away when Vice-Admiral Kelly arrived at Admiralty House, had a word with Wilfred Tomkinson, the Chief of Staff, and went in with him to see the Commander-in-Chief. Sir Roger, true to form, acted boldly, resolutely and, indeed, bloodily. An admiral who thought nothing of despatching a battleship to the ends of the Mediterranean to oblige a friend was equally ready to despatch three of his officers to whatever quarter seemed most desirable for the fleet. They obviously must not go to sea in the same ship, he said. He disliked interfering with the programme, but a delay of a few hours in sailing would have to be accepted, and in the meantime his second-in-command must hold a court of inquiry, get at the rights and wrongs of the business and decide who must go and who, if anyone, might stay. It was needless to point out, said the Commander-in-Chief, that the correspondence revealed an extraordinary situation in the *Royal Oak*. Quite apart from that, both communications were grossly improper ones.

Upon consultation with some of his staff, Keyes decided to postpone the fleet's departure until midnight. It would do a little, but not much, damage to the programme. At all costs the precious programme must be preserved as intact as possible. Weeks of work, streams of ink, boatloads of paper had gone into its preparation. This was his third combined exercise, and would be his last. The command had come to expect a set-piece of him. To have to improvise, leap across gaps in the programme, would throw the whole organisation into confusion.

At twenty-past one that day, as Captain Dewar sat at lunch in his dining cabin on board the *Royal Oak*, the yeoman of signals brought him the summons. His presence was required at a court of inquiry to be held in the naval secretary's office at the Castile (the Commander-in-Chief's offices ashore in Valletta) in ten minutes' time. Calling for his boat and for the Commander, to tell him to collect witnesses and follow him ashore as soon as possible, Dewar got into his best suit and hurried off.

It wanted an hour and a half to the time of departure –
the postponement signal would not be made unless necessary,
and then only at the last moment. Here and there, harbour
tugs were on the move, ready to go alongside some of the
bigger vessels in the less accessible berths. Blacksmiths
squatted on the buoys, forecastle and quarter-deck parties
were reeving slipwires to them. The last boats were coming
off from the Marina and Customs House steps with the last
privileged libertymen and Maltese stewards and messmen.
    A little later, the ramparts and the upper Baracca began
to fill with sightseers and the old yellow walls took on a
bobble fringe of heads. Some folk made their way out to
the breakwater and St Elmo's point, and others hired
dghaisas to go and lie in the very entrance and wave farewell.
But the departure hour of three o'clock arrived and not a ship
moved. And as soon as it became plain that not a ship
would move, when the tugs went back to their own berths
and the cable parties began lowering the cables over to their
buoys again – then everyone went home, the unprecedented
unpunctuality of a Mediterranean fleet operation was
eagerly discussed, and somehow, quite soon, it was being
connected with that comical affair in the *Royal Oak*, at the
dance – when had it been, before or after Christmas? Hardly
anyone remembered. Libertymen streaming ashore were
buttonholed for information. Since they knew nothing,
the wildest rumours proliferated.
    There had been a mutiny in the *Royal Oak*, it was said.
The seamen had refused to sail and were holding the officers
prisoner; a force of marines was being organised to dislodge
them. Someone had attacked the Captain, went another
tale; someone had kidnapped the Admiral; someone had

sabotaged the engines. Revolution had broken out in Italy, in Albania, in Greece . . . but however imaginative the stories grew, they tended to revolve round the *Royal Oak*. The most picturesque, and the one that travelled fastest and furthest (because whisper persistently linked Rear-Admiral and Captain too), told how Dewar had had a row with Collard and got his own back by planting a bottle of duty-free whisky in his suitcase and tipping off the Customs.

Up at the Castile a court of inquiry, consisting of Vice-Admiral Kelly and two cruiser rear-admirals, dragged out the sorry tale of pride and pig-headedness and personal animosity. Facing it, across a polished table in the sombre, marble-floored chamber of the most stately of the ancient *auberges* of the Knights, stood Captain Dewar, now in real trouble. Kelly was growing snappish and impatient. He was not interested in the Rear-Admiral's alleged bouts of rage that the Flag-Captain kept harping on. He wanted this officer to justify his astonishing impudence in criticising his senior and allowing his second-in-command to do the same. But Dewar was not readily browbeaten and he defended his viewpoint with warm, if somewhat academic, eloquence.

The court had already heard from Rear-Admiral Collard. He had been up before it during the lunch hour and had, it appeared, satisfied his fellow-admirals that his behaviour at the incidents complained of in the letters was reasonable in the circumstances though not quite normal. He had claimed again, as he had claimed as a young lieutenant a quarter of a century earlier, at the time of the Portsmouth ' mutiny ' court martial, that he was ' not in the habit of using abusive expressions when addressing men '. Under sympathetic questioning he had admitted he had not found in Dewar the friendliness and loyalty he considered a newly promoted rear-admiral was entitled to. Since hoisting his flag there had been one or two incidents that had displeased and disappointed him; he gave details, but without incriminating anyone.

Commander Daniel, left to wait in an ante-room with his witnesses after a frantic rush to the Castile, was not called until the evening. His story was a confirmation of Dewar's, his 'excuse' substantially the same and the court did not detain him for long.

The person mainly responsible for keeping the sitting going until late at night was the Captain of the *Royal Oak*. At one stage he asked permission to recall the Admiral and to introduce the witnesses he had had brought along.

" Why? " asked Vice-Admiral Kelly.

Dewar said, with some surprise, that he wanted to put questions to them all.

" The court asks the questions, not you," said the Vice-Admiral coldly. He went on to ask one: was it a fact that Dewar had on one occasion actually endangered his ship, out of a spiteful urge to put his flag-officer in the wrong?

The Captain indignantly repudiated the suggestion. He did not know, at this stage, what the court was getting at – the alarming situation in Grand Harbour a couple of nights earlier, when the *Royal Oak* went to the wrong berth and blocked the channel for the *Ramillies*. Collard evidently thought Dewar had known about the change in buoy numbers and had withheld the information from him deliberately. Admiral Kelly did not press the point, or reveal what he had in mind.

It was getting on for midnight, departure hour for the fleet, when the court rose. Now all the evidence had to be typed out and laid before the Commander-in-Chief. Dewar and Daniel returned to their ship with the news that sailing was further adjourned – probably until midnight Sunday.

During the next twelve hours the comings and goings at Number 13 berth attracted a concentration of telescopes from quarter-decks all over the harbour, and aroused much speculation.

To a flourish and ' Guard and band ', at ten a.m., Rear-Admiral Collard came alongside in his barge and shortly afterwards, in frock coat and sword and cocked hat, left for the fleet flagship. Captain and Commander, having seen him off, resumed their routine Sunday inspection of the ship's company at divisions. Very few knew what the trouble was about, why the fleet was still in harbour. Of the officers, few were in the Commander's confidence, none in the Captain's. A vague notion had circulated that there was ' a bit of bother down aft ' – nothing more specific than that. Those who took a quick corner-of-the-eye glance at the owner (Captain) and the bloke (Commander) as they strolled round the upper deck saw nothing in their expressions to indicate that there might be anything special about this Sunday. Nor was there, except for Captain and Commander – and Rear-Admiral. For them, it was their last at Malta.

Dewar heard the news, in a roundabout fashion, soon after Rear-Admiral Collard left the ship, from a brother captain, E. O. B. S. Osborne of the shore establishment, H.M.S. *Egmont*. ' Propose to assume command at noon ', the signal said. Another came from H.M.S. *Bryony*, the Commander-in-Chief's despatch vessel, indicating that her commanding officer, Commander Guy Warren, was coming to relieve Daniel at the same time. It was staggering news, received in staggering fashion. In their most pessimistic discussions together, Dewar and Daniel had never reckoned on being summarily sacked.

A formal summons to the flagship came next, significantly phrased. Naval messages from seniors who wish to see their juniors begin in a way that, to the initiated, explains the nature of the call. ' Request the pleasure of your company . . .' is purely social. ' You are requested to . . .' means friendly business. ' Your presence is required . . .' has an ominous hint about it. ' Repair on board . . .' spells a carpeting. Dewar's and Daniel's, from the Commander-in-Chief in H.M.S. *Queen Elizabeth*, read: ' Repair on board fleet flagship forthwith '. On their way across Grand Harbour they met, coming back, Rear-Admiral Collard. They exchanged salutes with him, the junior boat easing engines as the regulations prescribed.

Dewar was piped on board the *Queen Elizabeth* and Daniel followed. The Flag-Lieutenant-Commander took them straight down to the Commander-in-Chief's day cabin and left them waiting while he announced them. Each entered alone, to be confronted by Admiral Sir Roger Keyes, K.C.B., K.C.V.O., C.M.G., D.S.O., in full panoply: cocked hat with rich golden foliage, frock coat and epaulettes, a foot-long bar of medals, collar decoration and enamelled Star of the Bath, white gloves, sword-belt and sword. On his right stood Vice-Admiral Kelly, scarcely less imposingly attired; and on his left Rear-Admiral

Tomkinson, whose mild, rather unhappy-looking expression contrasted with what could only be described as the granite-jawed impregnability of his fellow-admirals' features. In this sanctum of naval majesty and *mystique*, the heart and hub of the Mediterranean command, the silence was awesome and the atmosphere heavy with solemnity; the only sound a faint *click-click* from a broad-bladed fan that slowly rotated above the Commander-in-Chief's desk.

In the briefest of audiences Sir Roger informed, first Daniel and then Dewar, that they were dismissed their ships and were to return to England that day. His tone admitted no argument and the Commander accepted his sentence with a quiet, " Aye, aye, sir," but Dewar spiritedly enquired what he had done to deserve such harsh treatment. The Commander-in-Chief stared at him but made no answer and a moment of electric silence ensued.

" May I ask of what charge I am guilty? " persisted Dewar. Again a hard stare, but no word from Admiral Keyes.

The Captain stared back. " I shall ask for a court martial, sir," he said.

" Then it will have to be on this station," replied Keyes. He held up a hand to discourage further comment and nodded. " You may go."

On board the *Royal Oak*, Rear-Admiral Collard also was preparing to leave. His flag was struck at noon, having flown for little more than three uncomfortable months. For the last time the Flag-Lieutenant came to inform the Commander, as he returned on board, that the Admiral had ordered his barge. For the last time ' Guard and band ' was paraded for him and a flag-captain and his officers stood at the salute. And for the last time, in this or any other ship, the St George's cross of Rear-Admiral Bernard St George Collard came fluttering down. It had been his own decision: at his interview in the fleet flagship, Sir Roger had been disposed to let him down lightly, had offered to let him shift his flag to the *Resolution*. But, ' for reasons wholly creditable to him ' (the Admiralty's phrase), Collard had preferred to go. He was more of a Don Quixote than a St George, although only those who knew him well ever suspected it.

At tea-time, having turned over to their reliefs, Captain Dewar and Commander Daniel left the ship together. The whole ship's company was on board, for the *Royal Oak* was still under sailing orders, and Dewar later wrote that at this moment there was a ' spontaneous crowding on to the upper deck ' to cheer himself and Daniel as they went over the side; while the Commander later revealed he had received a letter of sympathy from the crew, which asked if they could do anything to help – to which he sent a reply saying, yes, they could show loyalty and a good spirit to their new captain and commander.

Forty hours behind schedule, at seven o'clock on Monday morning, the *Queen Elizabeth* hoisted the general signal to proceed to sea in accordance with previous instructions and to assume the cruising dispositions laid down in the orders; and led the way out of harbour.

' The battleships were very slow in clearing the entrance,' wrote the midshipman in his journal, ' and nearly all were a long way astern of station. No exercises were carried out during the forenoon. At night a lot of rain fell.'

It fell also on the Sicilian strait, on a packet westbound for

Gibraltar and England, with ex-Captain and ex-Commander of the *Royal Oak* on board; and on ' Snob street ', Sliema, where the ex-Squadron Flag-Officer was settling his affairs and fixing up his staff in other appointments, and complying with the Commander-in-Chief's instructions to remain on the island until further orders.

' A lot of rain fell.' It falls at every tragic turn in the *Royal Oak* affair, defying seasonal predictions, recognisable before the case is over as a certain harbinger of ill-luck for someone; perhaps a sign of divine attention, too, as though the heavens are weeping for the vanity of man. The least superstitious person cannot help being struck by the co-incidence of omens that marked the course of the drama: the ritual onset of rain, the three deaths at the start of the commission, the number of the berth, 13, to which the ship was mistakenly led for the final break to occur.

The whole business began on Friday, the 13th January, in the argument after the dance; it was to die down on Friday, the 13th of April; and on a Friday the 13th in the distant future, after more than thirty years of silence, the names of Collard and Dewar were to be linked in the press for the last time.

CHAPTER IX

'The press have been scandalous'

'THE Admiral wished to make the Commander of the cruiser INSTAL A JAZZ BAND!!' (This in thick type and block capitals) – 'The Commander, who knew the spirit of the sailors and feared that his measure would provoke a grave incident, refused. His second supported him. Admiral Collard then sent ashore his two disobedient officers. . . . The incident shows clearly that the English headquarters staff is now obliged to take into account the opinion of the sailors and that the formidable weapon of imperialism, the British Navy, is beginning to totter.'

Not having picked up any French newspapers on passage, Dewar and Daniel missed this, in *L'Humanité*. Southampton, where they landed in mid-week, was shivering in Christmas-card weather and the newspapers were headlined BRITAIN SNOWBOUND and ARCTIC SNAP CONTINUING. Not a word on the *Royal Oak* affair; there would be plenty next day.

What was the rest of the news in the spring of 1928, historically so recent a date? It reads like something from a mediaeval pageant or tableau of classical antiquity. Parliament was debating the Zinoviev letter revival and the Government proposing further cuts in the cruiser-building programme, to whittle down naval strength to parity with the United States and not much more than that of Japan.

Whatever titles Britain might hold next year, ' Mistress of the Seas ' would not be among them.

City gossip was bright with boom talk from Wall Street, an era of prosperity forecast that would far transcend anything the world had known. Multi-millionaire ' Jimmy ' White had just committed suicide and Belgian financier Alfred Lowenstein, in March, bought the private aircraft from which he was to fall, or jump, in July.

The names of Epstein, Augustus John and Nevinson cropped up most frequently in the art columns of the newspapers, author of the moment was Erich Maria Remarque. Among the newer theatrical personalities were Noel Coward, Ivor Novello and Tallulah Bankhead. Londoners flocked to *Journey's End*, while provincials with money to burn sought their ' capital punishment ', to judge by the goings-on reported elsewhere, at Mrs Kate Meyrick's ' Forty-three ' club and ' Silver Slipper '.

With the words " Well, here we are," Lindbergh had recently arrived in Paris; the opening remarks of his fellow-countryman Mayor Walker of New York (" As Julius Caesar said to Cleopatra, I haven't come here to talk ") were going down less happily with a shocked French nation.

In that city (through which Admiral Collard passed) James Joyce filed a deposition in his lawsuit over *Ulysses*; in Florence (through which the admiral passed the day before), D. H. Lawrence finished his ' tender and phallic novel' *Lady Chatterley's Lover* and began an article for the *Daily Express* (whose contemporaries featured Collie Knox and Beverley Nichols) entitled *Is England Still a Man's Country?* In Rome, through which the Admiral passed the day before that, a quite athletic-looking Mussolini announced that all Italian males would wear straw hats from April to September, to assist a declining industry.

Italy, Spain and Yugoslavia, Albania, Bulgaria and Roumania were still monarchies (although Carol was but a prince and Madame Lupescu unheard-of); King Amanullah of Afghanistan was the current state visitor to Britain and his dainty Queen's remark as she peeped through the door of the galley aboard H.M.S. *Nelson* at Portsmouth – " I suppose they are all making dumplings " – sent a chuckle round the nation.

If, conditioned by the cult of breezy athleticism that characterised the Mediterranean fleet, Dewar and Daniel had looked forward to watching some big-time sport, they came home at the right time for it. Ten days away, on the last week-end of the month, was the great spring sporting festival of Britain: Boat Race, Grand National, England *versus* Scotland at Wembley. The White City was much on the sports pages – greyhound racing being the new craze. At Moor Park the golfing sensation of the decade was coming off: American Walter Hagen, with his four cars and forty golfing-suits, crushed 18 and 17 by obscure Englishman, Archie Compston.

Sailors of the sixties forget how completely their pre-decessors were severed from news and homes when they ' went foreign ' in 1928. Nowadays, in the Mediterranean, wardroom and messdeck radio and television bring word direct from London or one of the overseas transmitters. Then, the fleet looked on wireless as a capricious toy, a passing fad of Their Lordships, a quiet number for shirkers and playboys, that could never oust visual signalling. The captain of a ship kept his yeoman of signals at his elbow, and turned to him in many an emergency; often he had to be reminded that he had a petty officer telegraphist as well.

Nothing of home or world news was heard from week to week in a ship of the fleet, except for an occasional bulletin from Rugby, transcribed in amateur shorthand by a telegraphist in his spare time and pinned up on the ship's company notice-board. Only on a Saturday night, as a rule, might the wireless office attract a crowd, as the football results filtered over the air in a crackle of static. Nor were newspapers so freely circulated. Local rags, provincial weeklies, sent from home with the mail, might be found kicking about the living spaces, but airmail editions of the big national dailies were unknown.

When ships went to sea for exercises and war-time conditions prevailed, detachment was complete, because wireless silence had to be kept. At such times the fleet was suspended in time as perfectly as the fleets of Howe and St Vincent had been, when they ranged the Atlantic for months and came home to find their enemies friendly and their allies hostile. A hiatus like this occurred in the third week of March 1928, while Exercise MU 2 took place: a struggle between two powerful forces, one of which defended a base (Alboran) and the other attacked it.

It lasted for four days. Not long, but long enough for the immediate past to fall into distant perspective. To the ship's company of the *Royal Oak*, her new captain, Osborne, was just a fourth anonymous quadruple-ringed occupant of the ' cuddy ' and the compass platform; and jovial Guy Warren fitted neatly into the gap Daniel had left. Dewar's short reign was almost forgotten, the angry admiral a tale of the past, a sudden change of personnel ' down aft ' part of old history, dead as last year's rifle-meeting results.

The fleet's departure from Malta left a reduced staff at the Castile to transmit to the Admiralty a formidable wireless message consisting of several hundred coded groups, explaining the situation in the *Royal Oak* and the drastic action Keyes had taken to deal with it. The signal went out piecemeal, by various channels, which all faded and grew congested with foreign traffic. As frequently happened in that primitive telecommunications era, first reports arrived corrupt, in the wrong order, and made just enough sense to the recipients to bewilder and frighten them.

The local correspondent in Valletta of a news agency in London had no trouble with *his* despatch. Condensed to a stop-press item in a few British and continental journals, it had the Admiralty embarrassed, the Service clubs buzzing with rumour, and the newsboys crying red revolution before anyone could say what the fuss was about.

Late on Thursday, 15th March, at the end of the first day's debate on the Navy estimates, Commander Bellairs slid open the sluice to a torrent of speculation and mischief-making by asking his question in the House of Commons and making the matter ' official '. The timing, a few hours after Dewar and Daniel had arrived in London, and the knowledge that Dewar was a member of the ' Richmond set ' and Richmond a friend of Bellairs, led some, too hastily, to credit a story that no sooner had the dismissed officers set foot ashore than they were hob-nobbing with the press and making trouble with politicians. And although some naval associates admitted they would have felt like doing the same thing themselves in their shoes, others, who might have been valuable champions, were disgusted.

The breath-taking unexpectedness – and inexplicability – of Bellairs's question in the House seriously shook Lieutenant-Colonel Headlam, the Parliamentary Secretary. He could make no comment – and it left the press to make a good deal. REVOLT IN THE NAVY – MUTINY AT MALTA? – NAVAL OFFICERS REBEL – NAVY OFFICERS' REPORTED REVOLT – TROUBLE IN BRITISH BATTLESHIP – TROUBLE IN *ROYAL OAK* – AD-MIRAL'S FLAG HAULED DOWN – ADMIRAL ORDERED TO STRIKE HIS FLAG: these were the headlines for Friday, 16th March. What it meant when an admiral hauled down his flag was understood by few, but it had a fine Nelsonic ring, the ring of dash and cere-mony the landsman appreciated, and it obviously implied some disorder in the fleet on a scale worthy of the phrase. The *Daily Sketch* explained: Admiral Collard was the ' officer in command ' of the *Royal Oak* and ' a flag is nor-mally hauled down when a captain relinquishes his command '. British newspapers needed garbled technical information like this to pad out the story. Foreign ones seemed to have got more news and garbled it better.

Away in the Mediterranean, the fleets were converging on Gibraltar. So were troupes of pressmen, by rail and motor-car and even by air, avid for material and comment that would make Saturday's papers more confusing and alarmist still to the mass of readers.

When the ships slowly manoeuvred to their berths and H.M.S. *Royal Oak* was sent to anchor off the mole instead of getting an inside berth at the jetty, her crew groused about 'canteen boat' discrimination (she was a private ship again, and the most junior). But the reason was clear when flotillas of motor-launches clustered importunately around her and brash journalists even tried to come aboard – until the commander got hoses rigged to beat them off.

Vice-Admiral Kelly asked Captain Osborne for his impressions of the state of discipline in the ship. "Excellent," replied the captain. It could not have been better. But the next day or two were to see severe tests made of the instinctive loyalty and discretion of the British bluejacket. Gangs of reporters mobbed and mercilessly quizzed anyone going ashore with H.M.S. *Royal Oak* on his cap ribbon. "Did the ship really go aground while the captain and the admiral had a stand-up fight?" – "Had the crew or the officers paid for the jazz band?" – "Were Dewar and Collard henpecked husbands, who made their subordinates' lives a misery by way of compensation?" – "Had Dewar and Daniel spied on the admiral in his cabin?" – "Where did the sailors hold their protest meeting?" – "Who stopped the fleet from sailing?"

These surprising questions, drawing some surprising answers, were fired at sailors on shore leave, who were first puzzled, then amused, finally exasperated. One reporter found himself swimming, notebook and pencil in hand, alongside the mole.

No one could remember when a fleet had last been under such intensive verbal attack – or a ship, for this splendid assembly might have been anchored off the Falkland Isles, all but the *Royal Oak*, for as much notice as anyone took of it. Sailors who plodded through the glossy green gardens of the town to the upper bastions of the Rock – to dodge the press, perhaps – found the blue sky over the bay, and the blue waves whipped up by a fresh spring breeze, framing a superb panorama at that moment of history. The two fleets were met where Atlantic and Mediterranean waters met, and the famous old maritime stronghold contained more weight of naval might than had ever been seen in its history. Pendants fluttered at the trucks of ninety-five sea-going ships in full commission. From the *Queen Elizabeth's* maintop flew the plain St George's cross of a full admiral; and similarly placed, in other handsome men-of-war, were the flags of two vice-admirals, six rear-admirals and the broad pendant of a commodore. There, too, in a few days' time, would be the most distinguished seaman of them all, a greater personality than Keyes, with no personal flag but only a small blue ensign: Admiral of the Fleet Lord Beatty, a spectator in his ubiquitous yacht *Sheila*.

On the day the fleets assembled, while the Admiralty collected its thoughts and its cipher experts and debated a line of policy, the First Lord played for time in the House and managed, without giving anything away, to confirm the suspicion that the Royal Navy had the biggest problem on its hands since the Mutiny at the Nore.

Mr C. G. Ammon, Labour member for Camberwell, who had been the Parliamentary Secretary to the Admiralty in the previous Government, was early on his feet to ask for a statement about the disturbing rumours from Malta. Mr Bridgeman had only just received notice of the question and had made some 'hurried enquiries' but could really give no details yet. A report was coming through on the wireless but its text was corrupt and hard to decipher. He hoped to let the House know something in a day or two. Meanwhile he would ask members not to pay too much attention to sensational reports in the press.

Commander Kenworthy, Labour member for Hull, most talkative and tireless of interrogators, did his best to provoke further comment and whip up an argument. But Mr Bridgeman would not be drawn, would not be ' forced to interpret a rather obscure telegram '. And the House passed on to consider the Racecourse Betting Bill, which Major Glyn was introducing: all to do with ' a machine called a totalisator or *pari-mutuel* . . . a kind of mechanical bookmaker or robot '.

By evening the First Lord must have been wishing that the Service M.P.s who had got their teeth into the *Royal Oak* mystery would emulate Major Glyn's contraption, which ' did not yell at people . . . but remained quiet and silent '. They simply would not let him alone, and in view of the number of questions put down for Monday he issued a statement that night to the press: a court of inquiry had been held at Malta by order of the Commander-in-Chief Mediterranean fleet, to ' investigate certain disciplinary matters '. As a result the Commander-in-Chief had suspended from their duties Rear-Admiral Bernard St George Collard, C.B., D.S.O., Captain Kenneth G. B. Dewar, C.B.E., and Commander Henry M. Daniel, D.S.O. That was all. Any further developments would be communicated when the facts were known, for the time being he knew he could rely on the traditional restraint and courtesy . . . the press knew this part by heart.

Word got about that two of the named officers were actually in London and an ambush was laid around the Admiralty.

In the newspapers of Saturday all was speculation still.
Some did their best to comply with the First Lord's appeal
not to construct a great drama on an insignificant domestic
naval matter. 'There has been no mutiny and no court
martial', said *The Times*; but admitted that the publicity
attaching to an affair which Commander Bellairs had
'thought it desirable to call attention to' must be 'profoundly depressing to all who have the interests of the Navy
at heart. A difference of opinion ... which results in (a
rear-admiral) hauling down his flag is a most unusual occurrence and, whatever may be the outcome, is for every reason
to be deplored '.

Most papers carried youthful photographs of the three
officers: a sleek, bleak-looking Collard; a thoughtful and
almost romantically handsome Dewar; a boyish, wavy-
haired Daniel.

According to the *Daily Herald* it had been common knowledge for some time that ' the state of affairs in the flagship
was impossible and could not continue '. *The Scotsman*,
advising the First Lord that ' secretiveness usually defeats its
own ends ', pointed out that Captain Dewar had ' the
reputation of being a cautious, level-headed Scot, the sort
of man whom nothing tempts to commit an indiscretion '.
In Hull, at the week-end, Kenworthy told his constituents
the Admiralty had bungled badly (he had, however, seen
nothing yet) and gave his opinion that ' one cause of the
trouble in the Mediterranean is that there are too many flag-
officers on the station, with the result that they haven't
enough to do. So, being active men, they are apt to interfere in what does not concern them '. Kenworthy, as the

affair proceeded, gave more and more the impression of having been badly frightened as a boy by an admiral.

Dewar and Daniel spent much of Friday at the Admiralty, but saw no one because no one, officially, knew anything about them. After they had gone home – Daniel to his house at Purley, Dewar to his club – Sir Roger Keyes's messenger arrived from Malta. He had been sent off overland about the time that the dismissed officers left Malta, but had got lost and arrived a full twenty-four hours after them. When he reached the Admiralty the registry, where mail is accepted and logged, was closed for the night, so he gave his despatch (a letter amplifying the information contained in the Commander-in-Chief's signal) to a duty officer who locked it up in the safe; neither, because of the strict security screen imposed by Sir Roger Keyes on his staff, having the least idea of its contents.

Sir Charles Madden, First Sea Lord, to whom it was addressed, first saw it on Saturday forenoon. And by that time Mr Bridgeman had left for Buckingham Palace with Rear-Admiral Fullerton, the Naval Secretary, for an audience with King George V – who was seriously alarmed, but to whom they could tell little more than they had told the nation's press.

Denied an interview with either the First (to whom he was, as he said, *persona non grata*) or any other Sea Lord, Dewar went up to his old department, Naval Intelligence, and drafted a letter which he left with the Director. It contained a suggested press release that might allay suspicion; and Their Lordships, when it reached them, wondering perhaps at the effrontery of the man who was the cause of

153

the trouble in telling them how to handle it, made no use of it.

Few, in fact, of the numerous letters that Dewar and Daniel addressed to the Board of Admiralty over the next few days seem to have been taken seriously. But the one in which each asked for a court martial, or reinstatement, received prompt attention. The Commander-in-Chief had mentioned this 'threat' in his own letter, and advised against granting a trial because of ' the inevitable publicity it would attract'. The First Lord, however, was by now more concerned with his own position in Parliament than the Navy's feelings. There were distinct advantages in a court martial. For one thing, the whole business became at once *sub judice* and ensured his immunity from questioning in the House.

With the air of a man balancing a tray of delicate objects and preparing to make his way through a crowd of jostling, jeering spectators, Mr Bridgeman rose on Monday, 19th March, to make his promised statement. He began obsequiously enough, excusing his department for not being in possession of all the facts until the ' by-hand-of-officer' despatch reached him from Malta. He had asked, he said, on first hearing of the trouble, to be informed about the precise nature of the differences, and the findings of the court of inquiry, to which the indecipherable signal referred. But Sir Roger Keyes had sent back word that he could not telegraph such information because it might be misinterpreted. Consequently, the First Lord had been unable to make any pronouncement until now. " The careers and professional reputations of three senior officers were at stake, and hasty generalisations might prejudice their case."

So far, so good. The House listened carefully. When the approving murmur had died down, the First Lord continued.

The Board of Admiralty approved the Commander-in-Chief's decision to order Rear-Admiral Collard to strike his flag and remain at Malta; and in relieving the Captain and the Commander of the *Royal Oak* and sending them home. He had now instructed Rear-Admiral Collard to return to England: " he has been relieved by order of the Admiralty ". There was nothing much more to say about the case, except that ' certain issues important from a discipline point of view ' remained and the Admiralty was going to look into them by means of a court martial on the Captain and the Commander. The affair was therefore *sub judice*, from now on his lips were sealed.

Asked by Mr Ammon if he would disclose the ' precise nature of the differences ' he had referred to, Mr Bridgeman said, " No, sir. All that will be fought out at the courts martial. . . . I hope (the House) will not press me further."

But he was not to be let off the hook so easily. Opposition members angrily cried out that the First Lord was ' feeding suspicion and false rumour '. From the Government benches, too, dismay was expressed.

" Does the right honourable gentleman mean he cannot even say what the actual *charge* is?" asked Mr Erskine, Conservative member for Westminster St George's. (Ministerial cries of " Why should he? " and from Mr Lansbury (Bow and Bromley, Labour), " Why should he not? ")

Commander Bellairs jumped to his feet and demanded that the ' terms of reference ' be made public before the courts martial took place. The First Lord cautiously side-stepped:

" The terms of reference " (experts confessed they were not clear what was meant by this expression) " will of course be decided by the convening officer, who in this case is the Commander-in-Chief. I do not know whether or not it is the practice to communicate them direct at once to the press, but I will let my honourable and gallant friend know."

Bellairs: " Will the officers be allowed to be represented by King's Counsel ? "

Bridgeman: " Yes, if they so wish."

" Will the public be admitted, as usual, to the court ? "

" Yes, sir."

" What's all this about the *Royal Oak* ? " was the question in many a letter arriving from home, to sailors in the combined fleets at Gibraltar. The newspapers were arriving too, so they could read, if not the answer to it, at least the reason for asking it. At this stage, even on board the *Royal Oak* herself, the stories in the papers from Britain came as the first indication of something strange about the recent re-shuffle of senior officers' jobs. The coming and going of admirals and captains is to the lower deck almost as much of a mystery as the migration of birds, is not much more intriguing and scarcely more remarked upon. As for the journalists who infested the mole and the bars along the main street, their behaviour was equally incomprehensible, the Commander-in-Chief's prohibition on talking to them not really necessary, for what business of the Royal Navy was theirs ? A piece of impudence, was the lower deck's view, broadcasting ignorant yarns about the Service, with their ridiculous attempts at 'navy talk' – such as, that the fleets had 'docked' at Gibraltar. Civvies!

With the first phase of the manoeuvres over and the subsequent post-mortem in the coaling-shed on the mole completed, Admiral Sir Roger Keyes could devote more time to a consideration of his action and of the forthcoming courts martial. Beyond doubt, the Admiralty had an awkward situation on their hands – largely a situation of their own contriving, admittedly, the result of some extraordinarily ham-fisted handling at their end. Would they blame him? Was he wrong? To leaders like Keyes the 'rightness' or 'wrongness' of a decision rarely applies. It is 'right' to make it, swiftly and boldly, and then stick to it, *ruat caelum*. During the big 'At Home' the Atlantic fleet gave the Mediterranean fleet on board H.M.S. *Nelson* his old chief agreed with him.

"Thank God, Roger, you had the guts to do what you did," said Beatty.

Official reassurance came in the mail next day, Tuesday, 20th March. In a friendly letter, the First Sea Lord commended him for what he had done and agreed he had had 'no alternative'. That night there was another huge reception, the Mediterranean fleet's reciprocal 'At Home'. Afterwards the Navy's most celebrated ship's concert party, the 'Oak Leaves', put on a show in the coaling-shed. A too-topical joke was cut out of the script, but what was left went down extremely well. If Sir Roger Keyes, sitting in the front row of the stalls with Vice-Admirals Kelly and Brand (Commander-in-Chief Atlantic fleet) on either side of him, looked at all preoccupied, it was only on account of the weather having suddenly turned nasty.

' A strong south-westerly wind got up during the evening ', says the midshipman's journal. ' Steam had to be raised for slow speed, an anchor watch set and all the boats hoisted or sent inshore. After veering to the westward the wind died down.' The theatre-going crowds from the coaling-shed returned to their ships in a flat calm.

Captain Dewar and Commander Daniel presented themselves at the Admiralty once again that day and were handed copies of the charges on which they were to be tried. There were two apiece, concerning the contravention of regulations about (*a*) writing and (*b*) forwarding ' subversive documents '.

Both officers raised instant objections. The charges were ' artificial ' and had been drawn up at the Admiralty – in other words, Their Lordships were acting as prosecutor and judge rolled into one. Why had not the complainant framed the charges? Vice-Admiral Kelly's secretary, said Dewar, was ' particularly skilled ' at it and ' if a charge could have been framed, no one could have done it better '. Then the charges were too vague as they stood and would not give the accused a chance to bring in the evidence they wanted to. Dewar argued until he was granted an interview with the Deputy Judge Advocate of the Fleet.

Paymaster Captain H. A. Measham, though on the point of leaving for Gibraltar where he was to act as legal adviser to the Commander-in-Chief for the courts martial, spent an hour analysing the charges for him. There was really no defence, he said, cheerfully; ' nothing could excuse remarks about, or criticism of, a senior officer '. How then, asked Dewar, could a junior lay a legitimate complaint against a senior? Was not criticism inherent in the stating of it? No, said the Deputy Judge Advocate, the junior must confine himself to a description of the conduct complained of. He must not *comment* on it. This was the crux of the whole case.

Dewar went back to his club – lamenting that executive officers, unlike paymasters, had to learn their law the hard way by colliding with it – to appeal to Their Lordships. He seized on the remarks of the First Lord in Parliament, and quoted them (they were to be useful to him several times before the affair ended): " All will be fought out at the courts martial. . . . our chief desire is that justice shall be done and that there is fair play for these officers." He asked that his charges might be 'broadened', or a fresh one added, to allow him to introduce the matter of Collard's past conduct: something on the lines of ' For that he forwarded a letter in which he made unjustifiable complaints against Rear-Admiral Collard '. The reply came at once.

' My Lords Commissioners of the Admiralty have considered your letter of today's date in which you make certain representations as to the charges upon which it has been suggested to the Commander-in-Chief Mediterranean that you should be tried by court martial at Gibraltar.

' My Lords appreciate the point which you urge upon Them.

' They have decided not to recommend the addition of a fresh charge such as you suggest.

' They propose, however, to order Rear-Admiral Collard to Gibraltar as a witness for the prosecution to give evidence as to the receipt of your letter of 8th March addressed through him to the Vice-Admiral First Battle Squadron.

He will then be available for cross-examination by the defence to such extent as they may deem it advisable. It is considered that the defence will thus have an opportunity of eliciting such facts as they may think necessary.'

All this time the Rear-Admiral was sitting quietly at Malta, saying nothing to anyone and waiting for orders. When the Admiralty signal arrived he and his wife took passage to Syracuse in an Italian vessel and quietly boarded a train. The next signal, diverting him to Gibraltar, came over the telephone just as he had quietly reached his home, Blackheath House, Milford, Surrey. Just as quietly he retraced his journey through London and Paris, and took a train for Madrid and Gibraltar. Officially, the Admiralty told him, he was now on leave and on half-pay.

Everyone assumed that the courts martial would be held at Gibraltar, where a sufficient number of officers of the requisite seniority to form two courts was present (although the Atlantic fleet would have to leave before the end of the month). But the venue was not exactly fixed at the moment. Someone made a superficially attractive suggestion to Admiral Keyes that, in order to comply with orders and still outwit the press, he might stage them ' in public ' on board a ship anchored in Tetuan bay off the coast of Morocco, where only the most determined correspondents on the most generous expense allowances could hope to reach her. But the First Lord made it clear that, whatever privacy had obtained up to now, the time had come for a full, free and frank display of naval justice and fair play, a demonstration that the British Navy had nothing to hide. The Commander-in-Chief therefore chose the roomiest ship he had, the aircraft-carrier *Eagle* (these aircraft-carriers had their uses, after all) and made space for her alongside the main jetty at Gibraltar.

One naval wife who sniffed a spicy story and had no inhibitions about keeping the Service silent – her husband was a junior paymaster in the *Eagle* and her name was Ursula Bloom – raced out to find him worried to death over the problem of securing more chairs and bunting than the fleet could readily supply, and more coconut-matting than there appeared to be in the whole of Spain, with which to furnish the main hangar. A big audience was expected. No spectator holding a British passport was to be denied admission, and about fifty newspapers and agencies had already requested facilities.

Satisfied that the *Royal Oak* affair was dormant until after the courts martial, the First Lord of the Admiralty gave himself a rest from the House of Commons on Thursday, 22nd March. His satisfaction was not shared by all the members, in particular not by those who had looked forward to an afternoon's bear-baiting. What a parliamentary correspondent described as 'an amusing incident' took place when the House assembled. A Labour member with a long speech prepared moved an adjournment in protest against Mr Bridgeman's absence. Losing the motion he also lost his right to speak. But Lieutenant-Commander Kenworthy snatched the case out of his hands and eagerly presented it.

Kenworthy sang an old refrain: all the facts of the *Royal Oak* case must be put before the public at once. 'The extraordinary stories that have appeared, the extraordinary nature of the episode and its rarity ', demanded it, if nothing else. Were the 'terms of reference' of the forthcoming courts martial going to be comprehensive enough to permit a proper investigation of all the facts? Did the House realise one had to go back a hundred years for another example of a rear-admiral being ordered to haul down his flag?

When he paused for breath, Bellairs struck in from the other side of the House: " Will the First Lord state the respective terms of the charges that will be brought against the Captain and Commander of the *Royal Oak* and on what date the courts martial will assemble? "

Lieutenant-Colonel Headlam, peremptory by comparison with his more ingratiating and conciliatory chief, said the courts martial would take place as soon as possible and, as to the rest of the question, he must ask the House to show the same patience and reticence they would show if this were a civil case.

Bellairs: " Does that mean the two officers are proceeding to Gibraltar without knowing what are the charges against them? "

Headlam: " No, it does not. The two officers will be informed before they go." (They had in fact already been informed, and it is hard to see how either Headlam or Bellairs could not have known it.)

" Then what is the objection to informing this House what the charges are? "

" The objection is, that it is not the custom and never has been the custom to divulge the charges in a court martial." (Ministerial cheers.)

Shifting ground, the member for Maidstone asked, after some interruptions, " Will there be any further courts martial, seeing that Rear-Admiral Collard is reported as being on half-pay?"

These and all subsequent questions the Parliamentary Secretary played with a dead bat: "I cannot comment on that. . . . I cannot go beyond what the First Lord said the other day. . . . I have no information on that point."

It was the long drawn-out debate on the Navy estimates, now being considered on report, that gave the Opposition and the naval M.P.s their chances to intersperse comment and question on the *Royal Oak* affair. Efforts to bring the discussion round to the courts martial and Admiral Keyes's 'blunder' culminated in a reiterated demand from Kenworthy that the public must know the facts now, because 'discipline is so important, the discipline of the fleet so high and the case so exceptional' – and brought at last a reproof from the Speaker. It was the custom of the House, he said, to avoid discussion on *sub judice* matters.

But within ten minutes Commander Bellairs had led back to the topic. His opening remarks, that he intended to respect the Admiralty's request for reticence, prefaced a long rambling speech which clearly showed he had been well-primed by someone. He wanted to know whether the charges were based on the *form* or the *contents* of the letters Dewar and Daniel were supposed to have written from the *Royal Oak*. The Board of Admiralty, he said, would have to get its priorities right. To forward an incorrectly worded letter was a microscopic offence compared with the offences that inspired the writing of the letter in the first place. It was the state of affairs in the *Royal Oak* before the letters came to be written that the public was concerned about and, as far as Bellairs could see, no provision was being made to look into it – unless, of course, it was the intention to court-martial the Rear-Admiral in due course. But Collard was on half-pay and a half-pay officer could not be court-martialled.

" If the great captain of a battleship costing six million pounds," the member for Maidstone wound up, " cannot get his case stated with justice, what chance has the poor man on the lower deck? " That was the question the nation would ask and it might result in the whole of the Naval Discipline Act having to be brought on to the floor of the House of Commons. He warned the First Lord to have a care of the Navy's prestige. A captain and a commander had been publicly disgraced and sent home and humiliated. It was not good for discipline. In H.M.S. *Royal Oak*, ' that happy and contented ship ', the whole of the crew had poured on deck and rushed to the side and cheered their officers as they left.

At these revelations a buzz of excitement arose. Mr Ammon supported the Commander from the Opposition front benches and condemned the Admiralty's policy of ' Hush! Hush! ' from the time the first question had been asked. It was really expecting too much of the credulity of the House, he said, to claim that Whitehall of all places could not decipher a wireless message; if that were true it would be a serious reflection on the efficiency of our naval communications and a case that needed close scrutiny, for our safety in time of war would depend on them. What was the First Lord trying to hide? On the very day he told the House he had no information, the two officers were actually in London and had visited the Admiralty.

Sir G. Hohler, Conservative member for Gillingham, hoped the Admiralty would continue to keep quiet until the whole thing had blown over. M.P.s had no business 'bandying opinions about a matter of which they knew absolutely nothing'. Rear-Admiral Tufton Beamish (Lewes) poured more cold water. It was quite the normal thing, he told the House, for the crew to give an officer 'something in the nature of a cheer' when he left a ship. He suspected the motives of his gallant friends who 'burned to display their oratorical powers and pose as champions of the people' and used incidents such as this to create a prejudice in favour of one officer at the expense of another. It was about time someone put in a good word (he inferred) for Rear-Admiral Collard.

Half a gale was blowing, and the rain bucketing down, when the last units of the combined fleets left Gibraltar in the evening of 22nd March for a final course of night encounters and interceptions. Thirty hours later, at midnight on Friday, the exercises came to an end and the Straits were suddenly a blaze of fairy lights as all the warships switched on their navigation lights. From the *Queen Elizabeth*, Admiral Sir Roger Keyes re-formed the Mediterranean squadrons and led them back to Gibraltar. Vice-Admiral Sir Hubert Brand in his flagship H.M.S. *Nelson* passed the Atlantic fleet its dispositions and a course for the first leg of the voyage to Plymouth. He was taking his ships home for the 'little review' of 1928 in honour of King Amanullah.

The weather went from bad to worse. Even the mighty *Nelson* tossed skittishly across wild seas. The four older *Iron Duke*-class battleships astern of her pitched and plunged, burying their bows in the heart of the oncoming waves, scooping them up green over their forecastles and washing them off their sides in white cataracts.

In such conditions, the battle lines of the Atlantic fleet – what could be seen of them – flanked by the storm-beaten, up-hill-and-down-dale topmasts of accompanying cruisers and destroyers, made an inspiring sight. They were visible early in the morning of Sunday, 25th March, to the few passengers who had their sea-legs and were up on deck aboard the s.s. *Malwa*, rolling round Ushant, outward bound from Southampton to Gibraltar. Captain Dewar (who was not well and about whose fitness to travel there had been some doubt) and Commander Daniel and their wives and lawyer were among them. Their travel arrangements had been planned with a secrecy that would have done credit to an Ustachi assassin on the Orient express, but a fair-sized crowd had gathered to see them off. The press had swarmed aboard in force before the *Malwa* sailed, but had gone on a wild-goose chase after the wrong officers: another rear-admiral, captain and commander. They were William Munro Kerr, formerly commanding officer of H.M.S. *Eagle* and newly promoted to flag rank; Captain H. D. Hamilton and Commander E. S. Brooksmith; all three bound for Gibraltar and the *Royal Oak*, the one to hoist his flag in her, the other two to be captain and executive officer respectively, in place of the temporary Osborne and Warren.

Dewar nursed his feverish cold and got down to some serious work on his case during the voyage. He looked far from capable of undergoing the strain of a trial such as this would undoubtedly prove to be, but insisted he would be 'all right on the day'. Daniel spent most of the trip in conference with his adviser, Mr Day Kimball, who was his cousin – an American, formerly aide to President Wilson (he had been at Versailles in 1919) and now a member of the English bar. He was to defend Daniel and assist Dewar. It was Kimball's first acquaintance with the naval judicial system, and he had been unable to get hold of the *Manual of Military Law*, but he thought the Naval Discipline Act and the King's Regulations confirmed Dewar's contention, that the charges were ' artificial ', if not fictitious. There was nothing ' subversive ' in a letter from commander to captain about discipline; the rules provided for letters of complaint to be accepted and forwarded; and an error in the framing of the first charge on each sheet seemed to invalidate them altogether – the words ' which tended to bring into contempt ' had been omitted. It was like indicting a burglar for being on enclosed premises without inserting the phrase ' with intent to commit a felony '. Where charges were not sufficiently specific, the accused could not know what he had to answer or the court what it had to determine. ' This omission,' Dewar later recalled, ' seemed to us very important and when the anchor dropped in Gibraltar bay we felt confident of acquittal.'

The *Malwa*, several hours late after a rough trip and engine trouble, limped into harbour on Tuesday, 27th March. The accused officers were met by a staff officer from the Mediterranean fleet flagship with formal charges to serve and an order to issue, that they must on no account go on board the *Royal Oak*. An office had been set aside for them in H.M.S. *Valiant* (scene of a new passage for the history he had compiled long ago, Daniel might have reflected, if anyone were keeping it up to date) and facilities provided there for interviewing their witnesses and preparing their cases. They had little more than forty-eight hours to do all this. The court martial on Commander Daniel was fixed for Friday, the 30th.

Barely were the party settled in their hotel, the Bristol, than an embarrassed management had to break the news that the Commander-in-Chief had ordered them out again and into the Grand. Rear-Admiral Collard had just arrived on the train from Madrid and was heading for the Bristol himself. The transfer took place hampered by reporters and photographers, some of whom were involved in scuffles with the hotel staff. Someone fell, or was pushed, through a glass door. The irrepressible Ursula Bloom disclosed, while her husband frantically appealed for discretion, the information that Daniel was wearing a blue tie with red spots.

At eight o'clock next morning the crash of big guns echoed round the bay, lifting the seagulls off the roofs of the dockyard sheds and bringing some sightseers down to the jetties. It was a false alarm: only the guns of the *Royal Oak*, as Rear-Admiral Munro Kerr hoisted his flag and saluted his Commander-in-Chief.

One or two British tourists, lingering on for the supreme holiday climax of a seat at a naval court martial in a real warship, whiled away the day at the racecourse, the small elevated plain under the Rock from which magnificent views of the blue bay of Algeçiras, studded with lines of grey ships, were visible. Four thousand sailors were going through a dress rehearsal for the big parade of the morrow, Thursday, 29th March, the day of Sir Roger Keyes's farewell to his command; for, although a month must elapse before his successor, Sir Frederick Field, moved into Admiralty House in Valletta and hoisted his flag in the *Queen Elizabeth* in Grand Harbour, this was the last time Keyes would see all his ships together. After this week-end – courts martial permitting – they were to disperse in obedience to cruise orders voluminously prepared: the fleet flagship with the *Valiant* and the *Bryony* to Barcelona; the *Warspite*, *Ramillies* and a destroyer flotilla to Golfe Juan; the *Royal Oak*, *Resolution*, *Frobisher* and a cruiser squadron to Algiers; and the rest to different ports on the French and Italian Rivieras.

The importance of getting the two courts martial finished in two days had been impressed on the Deputy Judge Advocate from the moment he arrived. Otherwise, and once again on account of the tiresome trio – Collard, Dewar and Daniel – sailing orders for a whole fleet might have to be cancelled.

But worse things happen at sea, as they say – worse things than postponements, Admiral Keyes well knew. Their Lordships could so easily have turned nasty and made a scapegoat of him: a ruinous twist for one who was virtually First Sea Lord designate.

He had come through. His action was condoned, applauded even. He had a friendly letter now from the First Lord to prove it, a letter in which Mr Bridgeman seemed more anxious to clear his own yardarm than to listen to Keyes clearing *his*:

'My dear C.-in-C.,

'Ever since Bellairs sprang the *Royal Oak* affair in the House we have been doing our best to keep the ring. But the press have been scandalous and determined from the first to get something sensational out of it. If I had attempted to give any description of the affair from what we learned by wireless I could not have said much, and I might have said much that subsequently would have turned out to be incorrect – and then I should have been damned for misstating the case. When I wait, and refuse to give an account until I know something definite, then I am following the "hush-hush" policy and justifying the press in calling it a mutiny. And when they find *that* is wrong, they blame me for giving cause for suspicion.

'However, we are on firm ground in refusing to talk now until after the courts martial and the press can do what they like as I have no political ambition which they can frustrate. . . .'

The nearest Mr Bridgeman could bring himself to delivering a rebuke came in the last paragraph of the letter:

'It seems to us that, if only it had not come to a head just as you were sailing, the matter could have been settled without all this publicity. But it was obviously impossible to let them all sail together in the *Royal Oak* for the exercises. . . .'

CHAPTER X

Sailors' Farewell

IT was Thursday, the day of the grand farewell parade. Under the precipitous north face of the Rock the Gibraltar racecourse was a snowstorm of white caps as the massed contingents from the battleships, cruisers, destroyers and establishments ashore formed up for the march-past. Sir Roger Keyes occupied the front of the saluting base, alone. Behind him his staff and his admirals and *their* staffs were drawn up. To one side, among a small party of official guests, stood Admiral of the Fleet Lord Beatty in blazer and yachting cap.

It was as though the Commander-in-Chief had been greeted with thirty-four guns when he arrived, not the seventeen he was entitled to receive, for a perfect echo came back off the Rock after each round. Orders bellowed out over the parade were bellowed back by the Rock. To the combined Royal Marine bands' playing of a snatch of ' Rule Britannia' the Rock, after a moment of silence, played back an eerie encore.

Led by an admiral – L. G. Preston of the Third Cruiser Squadron – the companies flowed over the parade-ground, men in air-force blue from the carriers travelling among white-helmeted marines and the white-capped-and-gaitered sailors; ' eyes righted' at the dais and passed off for a grand march under the burning sun through winding streets, past the old white walls and stone gateways, the steep flights of steps and the shuttered houses of the garrison town.

When the troops had returned to their ships and the complimentary signals gone back and forth and, for once, a ' Make and mend ' piped, the day's excitement was not quite over. The local paper came out late that afternoon. Its editor printed also the *Official Gazette* and had been told to await an announcement. But none came; and only a few stop press slips, distributed during the evening, told the public that the court martial on Commander H. M. Daniel, fixed for the following day, would not take place. The biggest naval trial held this century was off – the news flashed round the world so fast that the missing sentence-end – '. . . until Saturday the 31st ' – failed to catch up with it.

Why the twenty-four-hour postponement? Everyone then was asking, many thought they knew. The defence had pleaded for more time to prepare their case, it was confidently stated. Persons best qualified to refute this suggestion (Mr Day Kimball, for one) did so. A newspaper-man got closer to the truth when he reported that fresh charges were being added to Commander Daniel's sheet. ' If this is the case, it seems slightly late in the day,' he commented. Whatever the reason, the delay could only overcharge the atmosphere still further and intensify the strain; and now a postponement of the fleet's sailing date was inevitable. However fast Judge Advocate and prosecution worked, they could not hope to get through two courts martial in one day.

The *Eagle's* working parties blessed the intervention, from whichever quarter it had come. They were busy making the large hangar look as much like the Old Bailey as possible, even to a precariously slung press gallery down one side. The fleet flagship, too, looked as though she had needed a respite, to judge by the orderly bustle of staff officers between her and the other big ships, by motor-car and boat.

An official release on Friday confirmed that further charges had been laid against Commander Daniel. He had not only criticised his senior officer, it was alleged, but had also ' published ' the criticism by reading parts of the letter to some of the *Royal Oak's* officers; and reading parts of the captain's letter too. This had opened up a whole new category of offences.

Two more big news flashes hit the Rock that night: an announcement that the Commander-in-Chief had appointed Captain T. F. P. Calvert of H.M.S. *Frobisher* to be Daniel's prosecutor; and (an omen of hope for outsiders everywhere) a report from Rugby radio that Tipperary Tim at 100 to 1 had won the most punishing Grand National of all time, in which only two horses finished out of a record field of forty-two.

At eight o'clock on Saturday morning the last day of March 1928, while the upper surface of the Rock of Gibraltar was still garlanded with smoke-rings of cloud, the sharp crack of a single cannon preceded the music and bugle-calls at morning colours, and above the ' island ' on H.M.S. *Eagle's* flight deck, overhanging the jetty, a Union flag went up.

It was the court-martial gun and the court-martial flag, the signal for a queue of sailors and soldiers and civilians to gather at the aircraft-carrier's gangway.

The first of the great *Royal Oak* courts martial, about

which so much had been written and spoken and so little was really known, was to leap back, after a ten-days' moratorium, into the press and on to Parliamentary order-papers on Monday. It would share the headlines with the Boat Race result – 'Cambridge Win by Ten Lengths' – and in the Scottish journals it would take second place to news of the most resounding thrashing administered to the English since Bannockburn, in the ever-memorable 'blue devils'' five-one victory at Wembley.

Many a London reporter who would have liked to see the match was at Gibraltar instead, along with French, Spanish, Italian, German, American and Japanese observers – these having to stay ashore because they held no British passports, but waiting in hourly expectation of scandalous revelations and a tale of bloody revolution, such as sailors had generally been the instigators of at one time or another in practically every country in the world except Britain. But the first of the *Royal Oak* courts martial attracted, after all, no vast audience.

Miss Bloom's novelist's eye saw a stampede and invasion of H.M.S. *Eagle* by all the British residents and an unruly horde of dockyard loafers and 'Rock scorpions' and a comprehensive cross-section of Gibraltarian manhood, from the fezzed brigade to those who wore their suspenders outside their trousers. Another lady, then a teenage girl on holiday, for whom the events of that day have remained as fresh all her life as though they occurred but recently, found herself sitting among 'only a handful of people, apart from reporters' in an atmosphere 'rather more solemn than that of a cathedral'. There were in fact only nine civilians present when the *cause célèbre* officially opened, and two of these were small boys who quickly got bored with the proceedings and slipped away.

The Services, however, were out in force. A Commander-in-Chief often makes a court martial serve for an object-lesson and a chastening there-but-for-the-grace-of-God-go-I reminder to his personnel. When, for instance, a navigating officer is tried for hazarding his ship, all the navigating officers in the fleet who can be spared to attend do so. No such suggestion had been made to the captains and commanders on the Mediterranean station, but most of them were present – a few in official capacities, the rest spectators, among about two hundred sailors and soldiers.

Nine post-captains of the Royal Navy, in cocked hats, frock coats and epaulettes, clustered into their places at the long table, stiflingly situated in the overhang of the flight deck, at the far end of the hangar. Their president was Captain Burges Watson, chief of staff to one of the cruiser admirals, and among them was J. F. Somerville, a future Admiral of the Fleet. A green baize cloth covered the table; on it, Commander Daniel's sword and nothing else. In front sat, to one side, Captain Calvert, prosecuting; to the other, Mr C. Day Kimball, K.C., defending, conspicuous in his grey powdered wig and black gown among the blue and gold and white of the uniforms that surrounded him. In the background, at a smaller table, with the official steno-graphers (two naval writers, sent all the way from Ports-mouth) sat the dominating figure of the trial, Paymaster Captain Measham, Deputy Judge Advocate – in the back-ground but very much in charge of the affair. He soon made it clear he was not to be shouted down by any Yankee lawyer. " Get back to your place," he snapped, when

Kimball first rose to speak and took a nervous pace towards the centre of the courtroom.

The court was open in the fullest sense of the word. The steel curtains of Hangar ' A ' had been removed, the sides draped in red and white bunting. Everyone sat *al fresco*, except the court itself, under an awning that rippled in a soft sea breeze and mercifully protected the spectators from the glare of the sun. Already, at eight o'clock in the morning, it promised to be a hot, sticky, thunderous day.

Down one side of the temporary auditorium ran the press gallery, capacious but overflowing. Royal Marine sentries stood at each end and were stationed at intervals along the route from hangar to gangway. The air was heavy – not only with barometric pressure but with a protocol and a ceremony that the centuries had hallowed. To non-Service visitors it was plainly bewildering but deeply impressive. Mr Kimball and Mr Charles Carrara, agent in Gibraltar for the London solicitors instructing him, seemed at first to be overwhelmed.

When the charges against Commander Daniel were read, most were hearing them for the first time. There were now four, the first two concerning the writing of subversive matter and the last two the making public of the letters. He pleaded ' Not guilty ' to all four.

The reading of the circumstantial letter – a description of the incidents on which the charges were based – took some time; the whole of Daniel's ' subversive ' letter had to be read in the process. Formal evidence occupied another tedious half-hour. The day grew warmer, the atmosphere soporific. The voices droned on. The press yawned and fidgeted and the spectators, awed into immobility when they

176

first arrived, were immobile still, dozing . . . until Mr
Kimball rose to cross-examine Rear-Admiral Collard and
everyone sat up.

He gave evidence standing, refusing the court's offer of a
chair, his jaw jutting out, one white-gloved hand resting on
the hilt of his sword, the point of which sometimes lightly
tapped the deck – Collard's only sign of nervousness.
Counsel tackled him first about the twenty-four hour gap
between the receipt of the complaint Captain Dewar had
handed him and his forwarding of it to the Vice-Admiral.
Was it not the practice to forward such a letter at once, or
send for the writer of it?

"In some circumstances, yes," said Collard. "In this
case, no."

Mr Kimball next asked him to read Captain Dewar's
letter, which had reached him at the same time as Daniel's.
The Deputy Judge Advocate objected that this was not
relevant, and, with some shuffling and tripping over coconut-
matting, the court was cleared while nine captains argued
the point. Resuming, Captain Burges Watson said the
letter might be read. When Collard had finished he was
asked if he thought the attacks on him 'unjustified'.

"Both letters were insubordinate."

"That does not answer my question, Admiral."

Collard bridled, squared his shoulders, glared at Mr
Kimball and said fiercely, "Yes."

There were sharp exchanges before the witness was
persuaded to admit that there might be occasions on which
a junior would have a duty to complain of a senior –
"if the complaint were made in the proper way and
through the proper channels," he stipulated. Counsel

asked whether Dewar and Daniel had at least 'acted honestly'.

" It was the clear duty of the Flag-Captain to come to me personally," said Collard. He went on to speak more quietly, half to himself it seemed, of the relationship between flag-officer and flag-captain, emphasising the word ' my ' – ' *my* right hand . . . *my* loyal friend'; ending, in a low voice, '. . . or should be.'

Kimball returned to the question of Daniel's motives and, after some sparring, the Rear-Admiral complained that he was not being asked ' straight questions '.

" Then I will ask a straight question: in writing his letter, did Commander Daniel act honestly or dishonestly ? "

" *Foolishly*," said Collard.

" You must answer properly, Admiral, one or the other."

The Admiral angrily objected. " Why should I ? It is a mere trap."

But the court ruled that he must answer and, after a pause, he said, "*Dis*honestly."

When the barrister suggested it was impossible for Vice-Admiral Kelly to come into the court with an open mind, because Collard had had the advantage of a long talk with him, admiral to admiral, the latter laughed contemptuously.

Kimball: " I am glad you find this amusing. We don't."

Collard: " I do. Because *you* don't know what you're talking about."

As the examination proceeded he grew more loud, hoarse and impatient. When his interrogator, dealing with matters in the early part of the letter, said, " Was that the occasion of the dance ? " – Collard barked: " Ask the writer of the letter." Told he must answer the question, he swallowed and finally said off-handedly, " I suppose it refers to a dance."

" Admiral Collard," said Kimball, putting one letter down and taking another up, " would you care to avoid a painful cross-examination by admitting that the statements in Captain Dewar's letter are substantially correct? "

" I say they are substantially *in*correct," replied the Admiral promptly.

But he elected to go over the letter, paragraph by paragraph, and this was the only time anyone heard his version of the main incidents. He gave a dinner party, he said, on the evening of 12th January and soon after the dance began he took his guests up on to the quarter-deck. There he saw some ladies sitting out without partners and drew his flag-captain's attention to it. Three dances later the situation was, if anything, worse and he asked what the Commander was doing about it. Dewar ' spoke angrily ' and he let it go with a ' Better make the Commander do his job '.

The band played abominably. The bandmaster was half asleep, taking no interest in the music, which was impossible to dance to. The conversation with Mr Barnacle went as follows:

" Bandmaster, what is the matter with the music? I don't think I ever heard such a bloody awful noise in my life."

" I am sorry, sir. I will try to do better."

To the Commander, as they walked away, he had said, not audibly, " I can't have a bloody man like that in the flagship. I must get rid of him."

The Rear-Admiral insisted to Kimball that no more had passed that evening. Was the bandmaster insulted? The witness looked surprised at the question. "I have no idea whether he was insulted or not," he said coldly.

"Yet you authorised the accused to convey your apologies?"

"I did not," retorted Collard with great emphasis. "Not in those words."

He had not known about the alleged uproar on the lower deck until eight weeks later, when he got the letters of complaint. He strongly denied, as he had denied all along, using the word 'bugger'. When first taxed with this, the morning after the dance, he suggested calling the bandmaster up to straighten the record on the spot. But Dewar and Daniel demurred and Daniel came back later to say that Mr Barnacle was not so much aggrieved at the language as at the aspersion on his professional ability. He had trained the jazz band as well as the Marine band – if he were told that the Admiral appreciated his efforts, that would mollify him. Collard authorised some such 'soft soap' to be applied. Everyone seemed satisfied and the incident, he took it, was closed. His relations with the Commander were cheerful, he had gone to the wardroom for a drink and entertained Daniel to dinner next day, but there was never any talk about being got out of 'a damned nasty hole'.

Reading on, Collard broke off to tell a different tale of the 'gangway commotion'. Dewar, he said, was the one who lost his temper. "I then turned to him and said I was sick of him as a flag-captain. Either he would have to go or I would have to shift my flag." Dewar 'argued all the way to the gangway'.

As for the 'studied insult' allegations, the witness said

that when he came off from shore the next day his valet was left to struggle single-handed with his baggage at the foot of the ladder. There was no officer in sight on the platform that projected over it and he ordered some men down into the boat to see that his suitcases did not end up at the bottom of the sea. He 'saluted the quarter-deck in the usual way' and walked to his cabin. Nothing there to make a fuss about.

It was almost noon when Rear-Admiral Collard finished speaking. For two hours he and the young barrister had faced each other. Now he sat down and the spectators, who had remained silent and intent, in a breathless heat, relaxed and shuffled their feet and sighed for a mouthful of fresh air. The awning flapped no more. The temperature was in the nineties.

Mr Day Kimball sipped water and asked Vice-Admiral Kelly to take the stand. From him he got evidence about the receipt and onward transmission of the letters and confirmation that 'a captain and his commander should work closely and confidentially together'.

The afternoon session, held up time and again by legal argument between defence counsel and Deputy Judge Advocate, lacked excitement for laymen. Some of the *Royal Oak's* officers appeared, among them Surgeon-Commander Cory, Paymaster Lieutenant Denning and Lieutenant Phillips, to describe the scene in the wardroom on Saturday, 10th March, when the Commander told them a court of inquiry was being held that afternoon at the Castile, and read part of the Captain's letter to them. No one had anything but confused recollections of the meeting, it was 'such a hurried affair'. Concerning the allegations of ' discontent ' and ' disgust ', Phillips said he heard talk among the junior officers but did not think the quarrel made much difference to the ship's attitude to the forthcoming inspection. Pinned down to state his own reactions, he admitted he was ' not encouraged ' by the Admiral's behaviour, but would go no further than that.

Mr Kimball spent some time establishing that the morale and discipline of the ship had been high and remained high, in the light of rumours that ' discontent ' had been one of the reasons for the officers being ejected at short notice. The temporary Captain and Commander, Osborne and Warren, took the stand and testified to the happy spirit of the ship's company; and a Royal Marine sergeant, the master-at-arms and a chief stoker followed them to confirm it. Before the last stepped down, Commander Daniel rose from his place beside his counsel and, in a rustle of awakened interest, asked if the chief stoker remembered the business of the three stokers who assaulted the petty officer. The witness did, and remembered also how that the Captain had told the crew afterwards that no one would ever be penalised for forwarding a complaint he honestly believed to be genuine, whether it turned out to be genuine or not. That applied to the officers, too, the Commander seemed to infer.

It was now six o'clock and the sun was dipping behind the white town on the far side of the bay. The awning seemed to sink still under the accumulated heat of the day. Few civilian spectators had stuck out the ordeal. The press benches were an untidy jumble of sweating, shirt-sleeved figures, in contrast to the smart rows of uniformed Service-men and officers below them. Kimball himself, a bundle of nervous energy when the case began, looked weary and listless as he rose to summarise the argument for the defence.

He spoke of defects in the charge-sheet. He said the 'subversive' paragraphs Daniel had added to his 'reasons in writing' were not critical of a senior officer, merely an attempt to give a picture of a situation. He pointed out that the King's Regulations justified an officer's report of such a situation to his captain, in fact enjoined it: Article 11, 'Every person is fully authorised individually to make known to his superior any proper cause for complaint'. He claimed that Daniel ought not to be penalised now for remarks that ought never to have gone beyond the Rear-Admiral's cabin in the first place. Regarding the 'publication' of the critical passages, what more could be said, asked Kimball, than that it was the only way of carrying out Vice-Admiral Kelly's order in the short time allowed, that all available evidence relative to the court of inquiry was to be collected and delivered to the Castile?

At six forty-two the sudden blare of bugles, sounding off the sunset call as ensigns were hauled down for the night in every warship, threw Mr Kimball momentarily out of his stride. The Navy's day was over and a moment of silence acknowledged it. But in Hangar 'A' aboard the *Eagle*, like a classical tragedy of old Japan that tortuously unwinds over a period of days, the long slow drama continued. From the ship's living-quarters, " Hands to supper " came faintly up, then the officers' dinner call, then " Night boat's crew, fire and emergency party, men under punishment and stoppage of leave to muster. . . . All the boys turn in."

From the battery of yardarm lights suspended under the awning, artificial gloom was diffused after the sharp defini-tion of natural sunshine and shadow by day.

On Monday morning, the 2nd April, Mr Kimball called Commander Daniel. Step by step they went through it all: ' dance incident ', ' gangway commotion ', ' studied insult ' and the composition of the letter.

Who saw the letter, apart from the Captain and himself? Only the Captain's ' absolutely trustworthy ' secretary, Crichton, said the Commander. He admitted calling all the *Royal Oak's* lieutenant-commanders, and the navigating officer, into his cabin, however, on the day he wrote it. He read ' phrases ' to them, gave them an outline of the incidents and said, " Now, for God's sake, stop me. Don't let me send this in if there is any doubt at all in your minds of its being true ". And one and all, appealed to individually, ' solemnly and definitely stated ' that the facts as far as they knew them were not exaggerated.

Kimball: " What were your reasons for writing the letter? "

Daniel: " I felt that unless there could be a total stoppage of such incidents there was no chance of preserving the morale of the ship. I was very reluctant to write it, in view of my pleasant personal relationship with the Admiral."

He went on to tell why he ' published ' the Captain's letter as well: on that hectic Saturday, at lunch-time, there had been a sudden scramble for witnesses. The Captain and himself had been given ten minutes to get their evidence together and attend a court of inquiry. Dewar told him to prepare a list of officers qualified to give evidence. He had

to assemble all the officers in the wardroom. He took a copy
of the Captain's letter with him, cleared the place of stewards,
locked the doors and began to explain, when the Captain
sent for him again to give him further instructions. When
he arrived back in the wardroom he resumed his explana-
tions, but was sent for a third time, for a third set of orders
from the Captain. On return he rapidly read the letter,
stressing the points on which the Captain wanted evidence
given. It had all been so hasty, so muddled and unsatis-
factory.

Kimball: "Did you read *your* report to them?"

Daniel: "I did not. I asked any officer who had the guts
to give evidence to come forward."

The Commander told how he was dismissed and how he
returned to London and paid calls on officers at the Admiralty. His counsel prompted the first sharp intake of breath
of the day when he asked his client to produce the letter he
had written ' to the ship's company in general ' on leaving
the *Royal Oak*. But Captain Burges Watson intervened and
asked the defence to consider very carefully whether this
was in its best interests, and Kimball decided not to press
the point.

Now it was the prosecutor's turn to take Daniel over the
history of the affair. Captain Calvert reminded the court
that Collard had had very important guests on board on the
evening of the dance, including the Commander-in-Chief
and Lady Keyes. When he started to question the Commander about the Rear-Admiral's attitude to the band, the
president interrupted and said he did not wish to hear.

Much of the afternoon's hearing, relating to technical
seamanship discussions about embarking and disembarking

in an exposed anchorage, was intelligible only to sailors. Coming on to the 'reasons in writing', Captain Calvert asked if this were not a 'rather peculiar' letter. Daniel admitted it – the circumstances, he said, were 'rather peculiar'.

"Did you not in fact disobey your captain's orders in putting your 'reasons in writing' in that form?"

"No, sir."

"Would you agree that at least you *exceeded* the captain's orders?"

Daniel would. He agreed also that by introducing 'extraneous matter' he ensured that either he or the admiral would have to go. He thought it would be himself, he said.

Why, persisted the prosecutor, had it been necessary to hark back to the dance incident when told to explain the failure to provide the proper gangway? Daniel, whose harassed, crestfallen air at the witness-stand this afternoon contrasted sharply with his breezy confidence at the beginning of the day, lamely answered that there had been talk in the wardroom of '*another* bust-up' at the time, so he thought it right to refer to the previous one.

"Commander Daniel, do you think the last sentence of your letter, with its reference to vindictive fault-finding, is a proper statement to make about a senior officer?"

"I submit it is another way of saying the Admiral had a down on the ship."

Re-examining, Mr Kimball gently elicited from his client the explanation that he employed unusual phraseology to bring home to his Captain the unusual degree of indignation in the wardroom.

Daniel had been on his feet now for five hours and looked

defeated. He was allowed to sit down – after Captain Burges
Watson had put one shrewd question: at the time of the
' studied insult ' was Admiral Collard in uniform or plain
clothes? There was a murmur of astonishment in the
hangar and raised eyebrows at the long green table as
Daniel grew flustered and confessed he could not remember.

After tea on the second day, Captain Dewar appeared
for the first time to give evidence, He looked pale and spoke
quietly, not fully recovered from his illness, but his confidence
was marked and his self-possession admirable, compared
with some who had gone before. Once again the ' dance
incident ' was thoroughly explored. In connection with
Collard's alleged keenness to smooth over the affair, Dewar
distinctly remembered the expression ' carte blanche ' being
used. Of the ' subversive ' letter Daniel had written, he
thought it showed a desire to bring the effect of the Admiral's
conduct to his notice, not to criticise him. The wording, he
considered, was ' not of much importance '. Answering Mr
Kimball, he paid a warm tribute to his late Commander's
' intense loyalty, both to superiors and subordinates '.

Next to the stand came the Bandmaster, the announcement of whose name aroused a titter, instantly suppressed.
He added little to the facts, but one of his cornet players,
giving *his* view of the ' dance incident ', provoked a ripple of
laughter – the first of the session, which brought a pale smile
even to the Deputy Judge Advocate's lips – with a ludicrous
attempt at reproducing the Flag-Officer's hoarse voice and
slightly affected accent.

A valuable ally for the defence turned out to be Commander M. D. Brownlow, president of the wardroom mess
in H.M.S. *Royal Oak*, her second-in-command, and, as the

First Battle Squadron's navigator, well known to and respected by every captain present. He winced at the unnautical phraseology of Kimball's first question: " Are you the *Navigation* Commander *on* the *Royal Oak*? " A peaceloving, taciturn person by repute, Brownlow revealed a defiant strain in his character today. Yes, the Commander had consulted him about the phrasing of his ' reasons in writing '. No, he did not think he had gone too far, he thought he had not gone far enough. He thought the whole world ought to know how high feeling in the wardroom ran after those incidents.

" The whole world? " queried Calvert.

" Yes, sir."

Both he and Lieutenant-Commander G. E. M. O'Donnell, the ship's gunnery officer, testified to the honesty and accuracy of the Commander's facts. There had been ' adverse criticism ' of the admiral in the wardroom; far from encouraging it, Commander Daniel had stamped on it.

The trial, which should have ended on Saturday night, was into Tuesday, its third day, when Major Claude Attwood of the Royal Marines gave evidence – in still more forthright fashion. He had once served on the staff of (and apparently suffered under) Rear-Admiral Collard. On the night of the dance he had been ashore at a camp, but had come off for an hour or two at about the supper interval and had been just in time to see ' something unusual happen '.

" What was that? "

" It was an episode. I had stopped dancing and the band had stopped playing and I heard voices raised, angry voices, and I turned round and saw Admiral Collard shaking his fist at the Bandmaster."

People couldn't have helped noticing it, Attwood went on. Guests stood round staring, then made a gangway for the Admiral as he moved away. That night there had been incipient trouble with the Royal Marines and he believed real trouble would have developed before a couple of days were out, had he not dealt promptly with the Bandmaster's request and got an apology for him and the band. He said quite candidly he had told someone what he thought of the Admiral.

" After he left," asked Kimball, referring to the Sunday morning reconciliation scene in the *Royal Oak's* wardroom three days after the dance, " did Commander Daniel say or do anything ? "

" He said the incident was closed and he remarked that he did not expect anyone to refer to it again."

" As a matter of fact, did anyone refer to it again ? "

" Yes. I did."

" And what was the result ? "

" I was sent for on the quarter-deck by Commander Daniel."

" May we take it you were reprimanded by him ? "

" It amounts to that."

Counsel quoted the passage in Daniel's letter about the officers being ' deeply resentful ' and Major Attwood said that that about summed up the position.

" Did any other feeling exist ? "

" There was a definite feeling that if something were not done there would be trouble in the ship, that it was impossible to go on as things were."

About the wardroom meeting and court of inquiry, the major had no real reminiscences. He had only had time to get into the boat and rush off to the Castile and then – he ended on an aggrieved note – his evidence was not called for after all.

The defence closing speech lasted more than an hour. Mr Kimball's verbosity, his unfortunately dictatorial mode of address, above all his American accent and landlubberly turn of phrase, were not the best recommendations to a court of naval captains. There seemed more than a faint antagonism in the air, at a foreigner, and a civilian at that, telling the Service about its shortcomings, reminding professionals about their duties. He came from the U.S.A. and he symbolised the upstart influence that was currently humiliating the Royal Navy in other spheres than this.

" I need hardly say," he began, rapidly and with nervous circumlocution, " I need hardly say that the incidents which it has been necessary for you to enquire into . . . are in one sense trifling, in the sense that you are looking at them as the origin of the exaggerated stories this chain of unhappy circumstances has brought about, but from two other points of view they are simply not that. . . . Your judgment must definitely determine the accused's career . . . and the word trivial is not the word to apply to the effect of these incidents on Admiral Collard's subordinates in the *Royal Oak*."

He improved as he settled down: ". . . If a commander cannot bring to the captain's attention freely and unreservedly every matter which he honestly believes affects the morale and discipline of the ship, to whom can he bring it ? " The action for which Daniel was standing trial was forced on him by ' *real* breaches of discipline '. The technical offences of reading extracts from the letters could

be ignored: they were merely matters of ' verifying statements '.

"Was there not something *wrong* with the *Royal Oak*? "
pleaded Kimball. " Is it not fair to suggest that the good of
the Service is involved here to some extent? If your finding
is ' Guilty ', so that all chance of reinstatement for the
accused is done with, will not the belief (which I imagine is
all too prevalent in the junior ranks of the Navy) that to
complain, justly or unjustly, is to get punished – will not
that belief be strengthened and heightened very considerably? I ask that you find my client ' Not Guilty ', so that
if Their Lordships see fit to reinstate him they may be free
to do so."

Captain Calvert, on the other hand, spoke to the court for
less than five minutes. Whether Daniel's letter was intended
to go beyond the Captain or not, it was ' subversive ' by
definition, and that was all that mattered. Whether he had
read it to other officers or not, or only parts of it, he had
admitted reading the Captain's letter, and that by itself condemned him. "Where is the evidence of disgust at the
alleged insult? Or that the ship was discouraged? Or of the
effect on discipline and morale? There is none, except of a
vague nature. I contend the charges are proved and that is
my final submission to the court."

More spectators were present than at any time during the
trial, and pressmen hung around the exit, waiting to get
away with their news, when the court reassembled and
Daniel was brought in front of it. He glanced first at his
sword – now pointing towards him – and then at the
president.

" The court finds that the charges against the accused are

proved and signed by the members of the court and Judge Advocate. Do you wish to hand in any certificates ? " said Captain Measham.

These are the testimonials every officer receives from each captain he serves under. Daniel's went back to the beginning of the century, to the old *Bulwark* and Lord Charles Beresford. Along with the names of all the ships (an impressive roll, evoking nostalgic thoughts from many a senior officer present – *Queen, Lord Nelson, Duncan, Victory, Excellent, Royalist, Dauntless, Valiant, Iron Duke* . . .), the Deputy Judge Advocate recited flattering opinions that commanding officers long dead had once held about this ' promising, hard-working young officer . . . zealous, capable and smart young officer . . . tactful officer with good organising ability . . . good disciplinarian and very loyal officer . . . zealous and able gunnery officer with great power of command '.

" Do you wish to address the court ? "

" No, sir."

Again the court was cleared, to reassemble with all the witnesses standing shoulder to shoulder behind the members, from Vice-Admiral Kelly at one end to admiral-impersonator Musician Guerin, the cornet player, at the other. The only absentee was Rear-Admiral Collard. Captain Burges Watson rose and declared:

" The court, having found the charges against the accused proved, orders Commander Daniel to be dismissed H.M.S. *Cormorant* and severely reprimanded. The court is dissolved."

Visitors not *au fait* with naval procedure had it explained to them that H.M.S. *Cormorant* was the name of the

THE FIRST COURT MARTIAL: (1) Captain Burges Watson; (2) Paymaster Captain Measham; (3) Captain Calvert; (4) Commander Daniel; (5) Mr C. Day Kimball; (6) Mr Carrara; (7) the Provost Marshal

shore establishment at Gibraltar, to which Commander
Daniel was temporarily attached while being court-
martialled. Dismissing him from it was the Navy's way of
saying that he was suspended from duty until further notice:
a confirmation, in effect, of the sentence inflicted on him
three weeks earlier by Admiral Sir Roger Keyes in the
Queen Elizabeth at Malta.

CHAPTER XI

Dewar for the Defence

THE mountain of naval dominion and power had gone into public parturition, and the result, so far, was scarcely a mouse. But when the crash of another gun marked the opening of Captain Dewar's trial, on Wednesday, 4th April, every seat in Hangar 'A' was occupied. Two magnets drew the crowds on board the *Eagle*: anticipation of the spicy disclosures that surely had to come soon, and of the duel between the Rear-Admiral and the accused, both of whom, on their showing up to now, were going to give good value.

In Dewar's court martial the *dramatis personae* were much the same as for the one just concluded, but some played different rôles. Dewar conducted his own defence, with Mr Kimball sitting at his side as 'accused's friend'. Commander Daniel was off-stage, waiting to be called as a witness.

The new prosecutor, Rear-Admiral W. H. D. Boyle, dapper and monocled, the very pattern of professional efficiency, commanding the First Cruiser Squadron in the Mediterranean fleet, wanted to know why Admiral Collard, who sat in the front row of spectators, was not off-stage too, since *he* was going to be called as a witness. Collard was asked to leave. Boyle emphasised this opening note of strict formality by asking that two members of the court be removed: Rear-Admiral Wilfred Tomkinson (who, as

Sir Roger's chief of staff, had seen most of the documents in the case) and Rear-Admiral Meade (who had been a member of the court of inquiry at the Castile). Captains Monroe of H.M.S. *Ramillies* and Bedford of H.M.S. *Warspite* took their places. The court now consisted of three rear-admirals and seven captains (among them Hamilton, who had had command of the *Royal Oak* since Dewar and Osborne left her); under the presidency of Rear-Admiral Townsend, the Admiral Superintendent at Gibraltar.

After briskly pleading 'Not Guilty' to his two charges (of accepting and forwarding subversive letters), Dewar listened to the circumstantial letter, then addressed his former secretary, Paymaster Lieutenant-Commander Crichton, as soon as the prosecutor had done with him.

" From your observations, do you think me the sort of person to lose my temper with an admiral? "

" Never."

The prosecution's chief witness was Collard, as before. Answering Admiral Boyle, he told how he came to be appointed to the *Royal Oak* and said he had previously met Dewar once or twice, but did not really know him.

" What were your relations together in the ship? "

" They were correct but not intimate. Anyway, I found it almost impossible to make friends with my Flag-Captain."

" Did you try? "

" Yes. But it was difficult to get on friendly terms. His attitude was correct, but there was no friendliness behind it."

" Did you place implicit confidence in him? "

Collard reflected so long that the prosecutor began to put the question again, when he replied:

" No, I can't say I did."

Admiral Boyle asked the witness to tell the court what happened when he received the letters.

" The Flag-Captain entered my cabin with a large buff envelope, placed it on the table, said ' Complaints for the Vice-Admiral ' and walked out."

" Would you comment on those letters ? "

Captain Dewar jumped to his feet in protest.

" In what light, then, did you regard these letters ? "

Again Dewar protested, and the prosecutor shipped his monocle and glared and finally said, " What did you do with them ? "

For all the lack of legal training and inability to get hold of the manuals he had lamented, Dewar obviously had a good grip on his case, looked rather more at ease than any-one in court, and was clearly not going to lean too heavily on his ' friend '. Now came the most dramatic and eagerly awaited moment in the two courts martial, as he stood up to cross-examine his former admiral. It was the first time since the ' war game ' – and how far away that day now seemed – that they had clashed in public. First he treated the court to a small piece of forensic ormolu:

" The justification of my action depends on the truth or falsehood of the incidents in these letters. I want you to help me elucidate these incidents— "

Puzzled, the prosecutor asked, " Is he entitled to say that ? "

Admiral Townsend told Dewar testily, " Let us have a plain question without any trimmings."

The shorthand writers exchanged a weary glance when the accused made it plain he was going to start at the very beginning. Captain Measham, as he had done at Daniel's trial, objected to the irrelevancy of the ' dance incident ', but Dewar quoted the First Lord (' All will be fought out at the courts martial ') and the president was silent.

From an interrogation in depth, Rear-Admiral Collard emerged unshaken with his own version of the story. Of the end-of-the-dance disturbance he said mildly, " As far as I know, you have entirely imagined that scene."

Dewar switched to questions about the effect of the incident on the ship's company.

" Discontent? " repeated Collard. " I have no means of knowing whether there was ' great discontent ' on the lower deck or ' intense disgust and indignation ' among the officers. Had there been, I should have expected my Flag-Captain to inform me about it. As he didn't, I take it there was none."

" If the incident of which I complained *had* taken place, would it not have caused great discontent and disgust? " persisted the Captain.

" I really cannot answer a suppositious question." At the previous trial, Collard had been nervy and irascible. Now he appeared to be quietly enjoying himself.

" Would not the bandmaster be discouraged and dis-satisfied? "

" I really cannot answer for the bandmaster."

" Will you answer ' yes ' or ' no '? "

" I will not. I will answer as I think fit."

Dewar tried again: " Imagine yourself – imagine your-self in the position of a bandmaster. Would you not be discouraged and dissatisfied? "

There was a spontaneous burst of laughter from the spectators as Admiral Collard replied very gravely, " I really cannot imagine myself a bandmaster."

"Do you think," said Dewar, " that a man of twenty years' service would have asked next day to resign if he had not been discouraged and dissatisfied?"

"I consider it impossible to answer that question," commented Collard, in his loftiest tone.

"A very *good* answer," interjected the president of the court, at which Mr Kimball looked aghast.

Over lunch-tables in wardrooms throughout the fleet it was agreed that 'Sammy' had put Dewar in his place – taken some of the bounce out of him. But in the afternoon Dewar mounted a vigorous attack. He had plenty of ammunition left.

"Admiral Collard, did you threaten the chaplain with a court martial?"

"I pointed out that it was a very serious thing to come and accuse me on a false charge."

"Did you say that severe sentences of imprisonment were passed on those who brought false accusations against flag-officers?"

"Not as far as I can remember."

He had definitely not used the term 'damned nasty hole' either, but admitted he had congratulated the Commander on 'handling the affair tactfully'.

The atmosphere was calm and amicable – the exchanges not the less telling for that; the two officers seemed at times to be chatting pleasantly to each other, on better terms than they had ever been. Dewar made reference to the walks they had taken, at his suggestion, at Dragamesti, and the

Flag-Officer's harsh voice softened as he agreed. " We did go ashore together on several occasions." But the audience must have wondered at some stages whether they were discussing the same incidents.

Dewar: " I suggest that, far from my being angry (at the ' gangway commotion '), I was extremely apprehensive and *you* were extremely angry and excited."

Collard: " On the contrary, I consider *you* were in an extremely bad temper."

" Was it not the *ship* you found fault with ? "

" It was entirely my *Flag-Captain* with whom I found fault."

" Did you not say you were fed up with the *ship* ? "

" No. I said I was fed up with my *Flag-Captain*."

" Would you be surprised to hear that a witness is prepared to testify that he heard you say you were fed up with the ship ? "

" I should say the witness did not hear what I did say, because we were standing well aft by ourselves on the port side."

" Did you want another flag-captain because the port ladder wasn't ready ? "

" No, I did not. There were many other reasons."

" Yet you said just now that our relations were perfectly correct ? "

" One wants more than ' perfectly correct ' in one's relations with one's flag-captain—." At this point the president interrupted to ask if this argument was getting anyone anywhere.

Unperturbed, Dewar went on: " Did you ever find fault with your Flag-Captain before ? "

"Yes, I did. At a dance on board the *Royal Oak* on the 12th January."

"Was that the only occasion?"

"The only serious occasion, anyhow."

"Will you tell the court of any trivial occasion?"

"No, I do not think there were any others. I was very forbearing at times."

Asked why he did not complain more often, the Rear-Admiral said, "My appointment was for one year and I thought we could go through that year without any break, provided there was a certain amount of give and take on each side."

Several times the Deputy Judge Advocate objected to the impropriety or irrelevance of Dewar's line of questioning. Once, when the latter protested against being ruled out of order, Admiral Townsend wagged a pencil at him and said sharply, "This court is quite capable of making up its own mind without your help. It is not for you to insinuate that it cannot."

"I most respectfully apologise," said Dewar. But when he in his turn challenged the prosecution for asking leading questions of a witness and the court appealed for a ruling to the Deputy Judge Advocate, this official blandly replied that the accused had counsel assisting him, and it was up to Mr Kimball to advise him when to object.

Dewar got the worst of a passage in which he tried to show that the Admiral's insistence on having the port ladder rigged was pure cussedness ('On which side does the Admiral usually disembark?' – 'On whichever side his barge is alongside') and passed on to a discussion of the incident of the following day, when Collard, returning from the court martial he had been presiding over in H.M.S. *Valiant*, had signalled his intention of re-embarking in the *Royal Oak* at a quarter to six in the evening.

"I arrived alongside in my barge," the witness told the court, "and walked up the ladder. When I had got about three-quarters of the way up I heard the sea washing heavily over the lower platform of the ladder. I looked down and saw my servant with the sea washing up to his knees struggling with my baggage as it was being passed out of the barge. I could see that it was far too much for him single-handed, and that if something was not done my gear would go over the side. Also the boat-rope had not been lowered to the barge and there was a fairly heavy sea running. Standing where I was I called up to the quarter-deck, 'Lower the boat-rope.' There was no officer in sight from where I was on the ladder. I then called the side boys and corporal of the gangway and told them to come down the ladder and lend a hand with my gear, which they did. When I saw my gear being safely passed up, I walked up the ladder, saluted the quarter-deck and walked aft, where I was joined by my Flag-Lieutenant. I stopped and talked to him for perhaps a quarter of a minute and then I went down to my cabin. I sent the barge back into harbour as I considered it too rough to hoist her in."

It was the same story, in more detail, he had told at Daniel's court martial, and Dewar had some questions ready.

"You say it was too rough to hoist in the barge. Will you admit that everything was ready for hoisting it in?"

"I have no idea. That is not my business."

"Do you think the Captain and Commander of the *Royal*

Oak incapable of judging whether it is too rough to hoist a barge in ? "

" No, quite capable I should say."

" Had you advised the Captain that, as a general rule, boats should always be hoisted in before proceeding to sea ? "

" I had."

" Would you agree that if your barge were going to be hoisted in it would be proper for your gear to be hoisted in with it ? "

" I would certainly not."

" I put it to you that there was very little sea running."

" I should describe it," said the Admiral in measured tones, " as quite a heavy sea for a boat; but perhaps you would hardly appreciate that from the security of the quarter-deck as well as I should appreciate it from my barge."

Captain Dewar, having at last got his Admiral on to the quarter-deck, tried to get him to admit that his ' studied insult ' in failing to return a salute had been, or could have been, bad for discipline.

" Nonsense," said Collard. " Discipline does not depend on that kind of trivial rubbish."

" What is your definition of discipline ? " – but here the court intervened again. The president had his own definition of discipline and Dewar must get back to the point.

" May I most respectfully submit," said the accused, " that a protest be entered in the minutes at the limitations placed upon the defence in the cross-examination of this witness ? "

Ten minutes later he made the same request, when told that Collard's interview with Vice-Admiral Kelly was privileged and must not be made a subject for questions. But he was determined to pick one big bone with his former Flag-Officer – the slanderous story that he had deliberately stood the *Royal Oak* into danger, the night she got mixed up with the *Ramillies* on entering harbour, out of a malicious desire to see Collard in trouble.

" Did you not, at the court of inquiry, accuse me of disloyalty which, if it had been true, would have been disgraceful behaviour on my part? "

" Oh, no," replied the Admiral. " I gave them this story to show how little help you were to me as a flag-captain."

A cross-examination on this incident, which was allowed to proceed although the prosecutor pointed out that it referred to matters arising after the letters had been written, found Collard irritatingly non-committal. Dewar explained that the renumbering of the buoys had been notified to the *Royal Oak* by signal, hours before the mix-up occurred.

" I dare say."

" I put it to you that the signal log was shown to you by the Flag-Lieutenant."

" I dare say."

" I put it to you that your signature is now in that log."

" I dare say."

" I put it to you that you saw the signal."

" I don't know whether I saw it or not."

" I put it to you that your signature is in the log, just below this very signal."

" The fact that I initial the signal log does not mean that I have read all the signals, or even any."

Urged to say whether he still thought Dewar had acted disloyally, the Admiral said, " A good flag-captain would

have drawn my attention to the mistake, would have said,
' You're sending us in in the wrong order.' "

" Are you aware that I advised your own Staff Officer to
send the *Ramillies* a warning signal ? " persisted Dewar.

" I am not."

But it was so, said the Captain, and it was unfair that a
court of inquiry should have been given a deceptive picture
of the situation. If dissatisfied, why had not Collard raised
the matter with him on the spot, instead of merely sending
for the Navigating Commander ?

" I was proposing to send for you, too," said the Admiral.
" But earlier that day you had left those letters with me and
I decided that any more fault-finding with you that evening
would have been injudicious, and that it could wait."

Collard stepped down. It had been a bruising joust, but
Dewar was going well and ready to take on another im-
pregnable fortress of an admiral, Kelly, as soon as the
prosecution had taken formal evidence from him. He asked
what the Vice-Admiral had done with the letters of complaint.

" I took them to the Commander-in-Chief."

" Why ? "

" Because I thought there was no other course open to
me."

" Thank you."

The inference was clear: the Flag-Officer Commanding
the First Battle Squadron had admitted committing the
offences with which the accused was charged.

After an adjournment for tea, the court called Captain
E. O. B. S. Osborne, Dewar's successor in the *Royal Oak*,
for evidence about the state of the ship after the dismissed

officers had left. He told it what he had told his superior admiral on arrival at Gibraltar, that morale and discipline were good; but added that the ship was 'not cleared up as well as it might be'; and Dewar, hoarse with exhaustion from long hours of cross-examining, could not let this pass.

" What do you mean by the ship not being cleared up? "

" I mean that, walking forward, one observed that ropes' ends were hanging about, or if you looked under the lockers you observed dirt, or paintwork not as clean as it might be."

" Did you ever go round down below? "

" Twice."

" All over the ship? "

" No."

Now it was the accused's turn to answer questions, at first those put by his ' friend ', Mr Kimball. Dance – gang-way – insult – the spectators now knew the story by heart. Asked about tittle-tattle ashore in Malta, the Captain described how his wife told him that several people had mentioned the dance business: " I gave her instructions to do all she could to hush it up, and told her to go and see a lady whom she had mentioned it to, and make her promise not to tell anyone about it."

Having taken a dig or two in the matter of his professional competence, he was able to get in one in return: he told Mr Kimball that he had impressed on the Navigating Commander how important it was to give Rear-Admiral Collard every help ' because on his bridge he was a little out of touch with fleet work '.

" Just as an example of what you mean," said his ' friend ', " could you give one illustration? "

" Yes. Going out of Dragamesti one day it was necessary for the Admiral to make a course signal to his squadron and he had to send up on to the upper bridge to find out what the new course was. I told Commander Brownlow that he really must try to let the Admiral know these things sooner, so that he should not have to trouble to send up about them."

Before the court rose that night, Captain Dewar announced the cheerful news that he proposed to call at least fifteen witnesses next day. But he opened the second day's proceedings by saying he had decided to save time and dispense with most of them. No one, he hoped, would take that as a sign of weakness on the defence's part. The truth of the incidents described in the letters before the court could no longer be seriously disputed. He expected the prosecution to reciprocate his gesture and ' limit its questions to the proving of the actual charges '. Rear-Admiral Boyle jingled his monocle throughout most of this, but made no comment. And now began a very long cross-examination of the accused.

Under it Dewar shed some of the cold composure he had so far so admirably displayed and once shouted, " I didn't intend to convey the impression that the ship was in a state of mutiny. You are twisting my words." He called Commander Daniel's letter ' expressive ' rather than ' subversive '.

" Exaggerated? "

" No. Expressive. Different people express things in different ways."

He appeared honestly mystified when the prosecutor tried a new tack:

" Are you one of the most senior captains in the Navy and nearly the senior captain in the fleet ? "

" Are these questions relevant ? "

" Yes."

" Well, I suppose I am. I don't know my exact position. I think I am about the fourth or fifth senior captain."

" Yes, and the tenth officer in the fleet, or the eleventh. Do you not consider that the fact of your making this report forty-eight hours before the fleet was due to sail on the most important cruise of the year would give an exaggerated and false idea of the gravity of the situation ? "

" As to the fleet's sailing, I have answered that question before."

" As to the fleet's sailing, that is not the important point," snapped Boyle.

" I told you I didn't consider the question of the fleet's sailing. I didn't visualise the programme being upset."

" Do you consider your action was promoting the welfare of the Naval Service ? "

" As things have turned out, no."

" At the time ? "

" Yes. What other reason did I have ? Do you think it was to advance my own welfare ? "

" Do you not consider that your representing the ship to be in such a bad state of discipline was a serious aspersion, even if made in an uncontrollable fit of temper ? "

" I don't understand."

Rear-Admiral Boyle repeated the question, in a louder voice.

" I still don't understand. The question is too involved. Do you mean I was in a fit of uncontrollable temper ? "

" Even if you had been it would still have been a very serious aspersion ? "

" Four days passed between the incidents and my letter. Surely the fit couldn't have lasted that long ? "

" That depends on your temperament, doesn't it ? "

Puzzled, Dewar could only reply that he did not understand the question. Piecing together the incomprehensible fragments of several like it, it suddenly dawned on him that here was a trial-within-a-trial; and that, in the minds of his accusers, he was guilty of something like condoning a mutiny. But the prosecution skated round this delicate topic and now, speaking about a sense of humour being important, Admiral Boyle quoted the adage, ' Laugh and the world laughs with you '.

" Do you mean I should have gone about laughing ? " Dewar bitterly asked.

He ridiculed the idea that he had led ' a Machiavellian conspiracy to get rid of the Admiral '. He had not approached Vice-Admiral Kelly or another brother captain with his problem – *that* would have been disloyal. " No," he declared, after weighing the question carefully, " I do not think my action was ill-advised; though I am sorry for the result. I never visualised for one moment the events which have happened, or that Rear-Admiral Collard and I would have been turned out of the ship."

Finally, he hit back sharply when Rear-Admiral Boyle returned to the question of his bearing during the period of strained relations, and the example he set to his men; demanding of the court whether it was relevant to discuss what might have been the effect of suppositious attitudes of his own. The court conferred, and the president announced that these questions were relevant, but that they must be put in a shorter and less involved form.

" Will this ruling also apply to the answers? " asked Boyle.

" Yes, it will, I hope," smiled Admiral Townsend.

But the prosecutor had had enough and Mr Kimball took only a couple of minutes to complete his re-examination. To sum it all up, what was the real cause of all the trouble? Dewar answered promptly: " Uncontrollable fits of temper – on the part of Rear-Admiral Collard."

And why had he never gone and had a straight talk with his Flag-Officer? – " I felt any personal protest would have been ineffectual. Admiral Collard would have immediately lost his temper and threatened me with a court martial."

Daniel took courage from his late Captain's performance and was outspoken when he came back to the court as a witness. Under cross-examination by Rear-Admiral Boyle, being reminded of St Vincent's words – ' It is . . . the indiscreet, licentious talk among the officers that produces all our ills ' – he said he had never heard that, but that it was most apt in the present instance, because the indiscreet licentious talk of one officer was what these courts martial were all about. He quoted in turn a remark he remembered hearing from a fellow commander in the *Royal Oak*: " He (the Rear-Admiral) might just as well have called my wife a tart."

Captain Dewar brought a new figure to the scene when he called Harry Goulding, the chaplain of the *Royal Oak*. Before taking orders at Oxford, Goulding had been an able seaman in the Royal Navy and had served on the lower deck throughout the 1914-18 war. He told how Band-master Barnacle had come to see him in a distressed state and had broken down in his cabin the day after the dance. He went to see the Rear-Admiral about it, he said, " not to make mischief, but to prevent it." But the Admiral had lost his temper and been abusive.

Kimball: " Did he send for the Captain? "

Goulding: " He made a dive for the bell but missed it."

" What was his condition? "

" In the greater part of the interview he was out of control. I had the greatest difficulty myself in remaining in the cabin."

Several of the men, Goulding claimed, had told him there had been ' an abuse of power ', that they had been ' very cruelly insulted '. He had heard the Admiral alluded to in various offensive ways, heard him called ' a bloody little swine '. Rumour had been so rife, and accounts of the ' dance incident ' so exaggerated, that he had felt obliged to warn some of the sailors to be careful of their tongues. Cross-examining, Rear-Admiral Boyle put one question:

" Would it surprise you very much to learn that some of the petty officers in the *Royal Oak* first heard about it from the London papers? "

" I know that is so," agreed the chaplain.

Dewar, who had handed over his case to Mr Kimball for a while, returned to interrogate his last witness. It was Brownlow, and the navigating officer gave graphic details, as he had done for Commander Daniel, of the wardroom sentiments. To Admiral Boyle's " Was feeling really so high? " he retorted, " Mine was so high I couldn't trust myself to discuss it."

The court now adjourned, in the middle of the second afternoon of the trial, to wait on Captain Dewar's closing speech. It took him two hours to prepare and another hour to deliver.

The prosecution, he began, had provided two strings to its bow, but only one arrow; in other words, the first charge against him (of forwarding a subversive letter) was contained in the second charge (of writing and forwarding a letter containing criticisms of a senior officer). Charges must not be 'split and expanded' like that; authorities on court martial procedure said so. The article in King's Regulations that he was supposed to have offended against referred to ' the doing of anything which, if heard by, or reported to, *subordinates*, tended to bring a senior into contempt'. How did this apply, he asked, when all he had done was to forward letters to his *superior*? Rear-Admiral Collard had done the same thing in forwarding them to the Vice-Admiral, and so had Vice-Admiral Kelly in forwarding them to the Commander-in-Chief. This must have been the first case on record where a captain was tried for doing something in accordance with the regulations. And the omission of formal phrases would have invalidated the charges in any case, even if they had been reasonable ones: the wording lacked the actual ingredients the prosecution had to prove.

Most emphatically he repudiated the smear that had connected his name with the 'scare' headlines in the newspaper that screamed 'MUTINY IN THE *ROYAL OAK*'.

" The idea of a captain of my seniority trumping up charges against a rear-admiral is simply absurd . . . if my or Commander Daniel's letters contained anything critical of the Rear-Admiral, they went only to the Vice-Admiral, whereas the criticisms that were being made of his conduct went all round the ship and were much more subversive of discipline. I view discipline as that reciprocal relationship between the ranks which brings about the most willing, efficient and intelligent co-operation in all the labours and trials of our great Service. . . .

" I also had to consider the spirit and morale of the ship, which is a real and living thing. There has been a great deal of misunderstanding on this point. We have heard the prosecution heckling witnesses as to whether they noticed any signs of disaffection in the ship, whether the men drilled properly, whether they were clean and so on. Last night I was told my letter was viewed as a frame-up, because in actual fact the discipline in the *Royal Oak* was quite good. Some clever people have interpreted my letter as meaning that the ship was in a state of latent mutiny. That thought never entered my head. . . .

" In view of the fact that I was ignominiously turned out of the *Royal Oak*, it is to be expected that I was guilty of some crime of conspiracy or disloyalty, malice, vindictiveness or even of uncharitableness . . . on the contrary, evidence has been given which indicates that I did everything a flag-captain could do to help his admiral. I admit I was not an intimate friend of Admiral Collard, but relations between him and me were quite good, both outside and inside the mess, except for just about two days during that band incident and after the 5th of March. Several members of the court will have seen me with Admiral Collard on different occasions and will know my relations with him were quite good and quite friendly.

"I treated Admiral Collard as an honoured guest of the ship. But how could I hope to maintain my authority if he attacked me in this way? Being convinced these incidents had to stop, what was I to do? If I went to him I knew I should be bullied. I might have gone privately to the Vice-Admiral, but I do not believe in creeping up back stairs. . . .

"It was certainly not to my advantage," continued Dewar (and now the rain smartly pattered on the screens outside the hangar), "to bring a complaint against my Rear-Admiral. I bore no malice against him. I bear none now. I am extremely sorry for him, and feel that nothing he has done deserves this scandal that the case holds to his name. At the same time, he has brought many charges against me. Only last night I heard from a senior officer that I am supposed to have worked with Commander Daniel to hunt the Rear-Admiral out of the ship. I have been told other things which, if true, would be a disgrace to the uniform I wear. Serious charges have been brought against me, about which I knew nothing. Now, for the first time, I understand why I was sent home in disgrace."

Again Dewar recapitulated the circumstances in which both Commander Daniel's letter and his own were written; his motives and the articles in the King's Regulations under which they were framed. His voice was louder and more confident now, competing with the gusting of the wind around the hangar and the periodical pistol-shot slatting of some nearby awning.

"I was ignominiously turned out of my ship," he repeated, "and within a few hours was on my way to England without knowing what I had done wrong. After thirty years entirely devoted to the Service, my character and reputation are ruined without a single charge being preferred against me. It was I who pressed for a court martial, and a broad charge . . . I am now before you on the trivial charge of having failed sufficiently to censor a letter. . . . I submit there is absolutely no case against me."

He concluded: " A great question of justice and principle is involved. I ask the court not only to acquit me, but to acquit me honourably. This case is one, sir, which affects my personal honour."

It was six o'clock. Dewar had been speaking since five, swiftly, fluently and with impressive conviction and sincerity. When he rose the *levante* had risen too and begun to ruffle the awnings, and a bank of cloud had swept down from the Rock and blotted out the sun. As he came to his peroration, a storm of rain drummed on the hangar, soaked the crimson and white bunting of the side-screens and cascaded down the scuppers. His closing words were almost drowned in the noise of wind and torrent. And just after he sat down a bugle blew a mournful call. He stood again, as though to a summons, and everyone stood with him and faced aft. Officers saluted. A half-gale carried the bugle-notes of ' Sunset ' across the bay, and an oilskinned signalman hauled down a sodden white ensign in sheets of rain.

The prosecution, as before, took about five minutes to sum up. Rear-Admiral Collard's behaviour had nothing to do with the charges, said Boyle. When he found fault, as he had a perfect right to do, he rightly called for the ' reasons in writing ' of the officer he supposed to be at fault.

" The rendering of ' reasons in writing ' is a well-estab-lished custom. It has for its object the avoidance of heated discussion, to give the junior an opportunity for explanation and the senior a chance to consider that explanation when the heat of the moment has passed. It is in fact the surest way to avoid a scene."

But the accused had used such a letter, addressed to himself, as the basis of a general complaint against his superior, in which previous incidents and problematical consequences were introduced. This might, even so, have been a mere technical offence; but in matters like this " the harm is caused by the way things are done more than by the actions themselves ". Dewar's plea of justification was an admission of guilt. His own statements condemned him. More deliberate reflection on his part might have avoided much unpleasant notoriety.

" I submit," was Rear-Admiral Boyle's last word, " that anyone who had the welfare of the Service at heart would have restrained himself a little longer, and forwarded a proper letter of ' reasons in writing ', and quietly made known his own cause of complaint at a later and more convenient date."

A twenty-minute adjournment was sufficient to decide the court. Dewar looked at his sword and saw that he was guilty. On the first charge only, announced the Deputy Judge Advocate, that of forwarding his executive officer's subversive letter. " The second charge is not proved and the accused is therefore acquitted of it."

Dewar put in his certificates. They went back in time to that blackened, whitened and buffed sepulchre, H.M.S. *Hawke*, and the sailing ship *Volage*, back to 1895: ' Served with sobriety and entirely to my satisfaction . . . a capable officer and promises well . . . a good officer in every way

. . . a very clever and hardworking officer whom I hope to see promoted soon . . . an officer of excellent judgment who will do well in the higher ranks of the Service . . .' (this was Richmond's prophecy). The comments of past captains on a younger Dewar sounded ironical today.

He declined to address the court.

The sentence was the same as Daniel's: dismissed his ship and severely reprimanded. " Officers convicted of drunkenness on duty, of losing their ships by negligence and of wilful disobedience of orders often receive lighter sentences," was his characteristic comment long afterwards.

When the findings were announced, two ladies in the spectators' seats dabbed at tears with their handkerchiefs. A murmur went round the rest – of approval at the verdict, or disapproval, or sympathy with the Captain; probably the last. For the accused's dignity and self-control, maintained to the very end, were what spectators remembered best in years to come about the *Royal Oak* courts martial.

Captain Dewar gave notice of appeal. In London, as soon as the verdict arrived, Lieutenant-Commander Kenworthy told the press he would be asking questions in Parliament after the Easter recess, about the two officers' futures and a revision of the Navy's rules for stating complaints; and that if he got no satisfaction he would raise the matter on the Navy estimates. Surely no First Lord ever prayed to have the Navy estimates over and done with as did Mr Bridgeman in 1928.

On board H.M.S. *Eagle* the duty watch of seamen began restoring Hangar ' A ' to its proper function. The chairs and the coconut-matting went back to the ships they had been borrowed from. The press gallery came down, the marine sentries fell out, the officers of the court slipped down to the wardroom for a glass before dinner. The *Eagle's* commander saw the last civilian – a journalist – ashore, almost hustled ashore, and went to tell the captain that the ship was ' rid of ' visitors, as he might have spoken of her being ' rid of ' a plague of cockroaches.

CHAPTER XII

The End of the Affair

BLOW-BY-BLOW accounts of the trials had filled page upon page of many British newspapers. As the sad, trifling tale unfolded – a swear-word at a dance, an argument about a ladder, a salute not given or not seen to be given – the nation sighed with relief, and was staggered that men invested with such majesty and responsibility had been led astray by passion so ordinary, that all the Navy's superb ceremonial had been engaged by a matter of so little moment. Looking down from the Rock on the anchored armada of British warships, while the courts martial dragged on, someone had jerked a disparaging thumb at the proud Mediterranean fleet and pointed out that it had ' only needed a stroke of a pen to keep that little lot in harbour '.

Where was the ' Mutiny in the Fleet ' some newspapers had been promising? ' Three Men in a Boat ' was more like it. European correspondents, having believed to the end that a major scandal had to break, retired bewildered. The journal that had promised the dissolution of the British Navy, followed by the dissolution of the British Empire, now confessed its respect for an Admiralty that had been determined to wash its dirty linen in public and been unable to produce more than ' a slightly crumpled pocket-handker-chief '. As though they had not been impressed and baffled enough by what one paper called ' these Thespian disclosures ', the foreign press contingent was now faced with the inexplicable behaviour of the principals.

After dinner on the evening the second trial ended, Captain Dewar went along to the *Queen Elizabeth* and had a drink with his Commander-in-Chief. Early next morning he went up to the Hotel Bristol and found Rear-Admiral Collard in the lounge reading a novel. Reporters saw them chatting quite peaceably, displaying, now it was too late, all the friendliness each had missed in the other, drinking coffee and after about half an hour shaking hands and parting on, as a paper put it, ' the most cordial terms '. There was no rancour now. The battle had been won and lost – or, rather, lost and lost.

Admiral Collard maintained his strict ' No comment' line and Dewar spoke for them both: " The affair is over. We hope it will be forgotten as speedily as possible. We hope it will not be carried on by other persons in arenas of controversy to which it does not belong."

Commander Daniel arrived at the Hotel Bristol later in the forenoon, by invitation; but he was late, the Admiral had left for England and the commander had to be content with writing him a letter of farewell on the hotel note-paper.

The fight was soon on again, in other ' arenas '. According to present-day recollections of those times (or perhaps recollections of what they read in the press), young sailors went through a ' period of bewilderment ' and young officers' reactions, if those in the First Battle Squadron were typical, varied between ' a sense of intolerable humiliation ' and ' a vague resentment '.

Public, or at least press, indignation burned brightly over

the Easter week-end. 'The dreadful treatment meted out to two high-ranking officers makes us think there isn't much justice to be had', wrote a Serviceman. Old salts, nursing ancient grievances, told the popular papers that the verdicts at Gibraltar were in keeping with the 'system of intimidation' the Navy called discipline; that if the officers had been ratings they would have known that to ask for a court martial was to 'ask for it' indeed; that it made a nice change to see 'some of the much-beringed autocrats get a stiff dose of the theory that the Navy is never so much in the right as when it is in the wrong' (this last from 'One who has Suffered ').

The Socialist press found the affair a godsend – a general election was not far off – and disseminated some imaginative opinions. One leading article said:

'The findings seem to mean that officers are entitled to behave to their subordinates as Admiral Collard was stated to have been in the habit of behaving . . . if that is the Rule of the Navy the sooner it is changed the better '.

There were references to the armed forces' ' pre-historic notions of discipline'; an attempt to raise a 'lightning petition' to the King, or the Prime Minister, for clemency towards the two 'unjustly' dismissed officers. Enough of the Portsmouth 'mutiny' story was revived to convince some readers that the Rear-Admiral habitually called his sailors ' dogs '. The *Daily Herald* wanted to know how soon ' another Charles Reade ' would appear, to look at other injustices in the armed forces, especially in their detention barracks and military prisons; and how much longer the British taxpayer and working man would be expected to provide jazz bands for wealthy officers.

A *Daily Mail* reader threatened that, if the sentences on Dewar and Daniel were not quashed, she would not allow her son to enter the Navy. This, said *Punch*, ' places the Admiralty in a very awkward quandary '.

The *Daily Sketch*, however, commented ' If a naval crisis occurs every time a senior officer employs a more vigorous expression than " Bother " or " Tut-tut " we are in for a fine series of comic opera episodes '; and one small voice – that of Major-General Hutchison, the chief Liberal whip – actually spoke up for the ' villain ': " I doubt if the British public realises how much Admiral Collard has suffered," he told a press meeting.

Who, or what, was the real ' villain '? The mob thought Collard, without a doubt, for his foul temper and despotic ways. But an opinion survey among folk whose opinions were worth having might have elicited as many villains as interviewees. There was Dewar, for a start: ' tactless, too outspoken, no sense of humour '. There was Daniel, who ' couldn't take a " rocket " '; Admiral Kelly, who failed to settle it in the squadron; Admiral Keyes, who took high-handed action on the spur of the moment; Bellairs, M.P., who cried it up in the House – no end of candidates for obloquy on some score. In the Navy, many were inclined to blame the Admiralty, above all, for making a hash of the publicity it attracted.

The Services, on the whole, made nothing of the incomprehensible fuss over the verdicts in the papers; they surprised no experienced member of His Majesty's forces. No one expected to do what Dewar and Daniel had done and get away with it: " If a senior and a junior have a row, the junior is wrong in every conceivable set of circumstances,

otherwise discipline cannot go on," Lord Charles Beresford
had said years before, and it still held true.

The *Naval Review*, taking no official stand on the *Royal
Oak* affair, had an apposite piece of Beresfordese inserted
without comment in the spring number: 'That's where
you're wrong, Mr Midshipman; Loyalty begins at the top
and it works downwards – *Not* upwards'. A cryptic *credo*
followed it, in which some detected the pontifical style of
Admiral Richmond:

' I believe in one Captain who commands a Ship . . . he
must be Lord of all within that Ship . . . the Admiral shall
be loyal to his Captains and protect them . . . the Commander-in-Chief shall be loyal to his Admirals, and take
care there be no violation of the sacredness of the Commands
of the Admirals in their Squadrons, nor of the Captains in
their Ships. . . .'

Leading articles and letters in British newspapers ousted
seasonal essays on holy days and holidays and first-cuckoo
reports. *The Times* article, expressing what its writer
(himself a rear-admiral) hoped would be an epitaph for the
whole business, spoke of the general feeling of thankfulness
that it was all over, among the ' regret and astonishment,
sharpened with impatience ' with which the verdicts had
been received. Three officers of ' high professional competence ' had had their careers interrupted, if not wrecked
altogether; but this was only one item on the debit side of
an affair that had profited no public or private interest.

Clashes of temperament, said *The Times*, were found in
every walk of life – the regiment, the factory, even the home.
But somehow they were kept in check, subdued to the
practical necessities of the day. Who, or what, had been to

blame? Like everyone else, *The Times* asked the question.
Whoever had put those officers in that situation, it seemed to
imply: an admiral too much addicted to 'the choleric
word' and a captain and commander too dour or straitlaced to take a perspective view of a passing tiff: a situation
that offered 'too little gravity on the one side, too much
solemnity on the other'.

While Dewar's appeal was being considered (the Admiralty dismissed it in the end, saying that Captain Measham
had run the case with great ability and conspicuous fairness
– and hinting there might still be a place for Dewar in the
Navy if he behaved), his champions Bellairs and Kenworthy,
one from each side of the House, were thrashing out the
trials in Parliament. The First Lord gave them their opportunity with a long statement immediately after Easter.

Although the Commander-in-Chief Mediterranean's
action of 10th March had been taken without his knowledge
or approval, he said, he and the Board of Admiralty con-
curred with it. Two of the dismissed officers had now had
the courts martial they had asked for and had been duly
convicted. (They should therefore be quite satisfied, he
seemed to say.) The charges had of course been purely
technical ones and the real offences an inability, or un-
willingness, to show give and take and to keep a sense of
proportion.

The trials had, however, exposed defects in the character
of a third officer:

' The initial blame rested on Rear-Admiral Collard, who
dealt with trivial causes for dissatisfaction in a manner
unbecoming his position; and showed himself unfitted to

hold further high command. . . . The Board has decided with regret, in spite of his past good services, to place him at once on the retired list.'

Kenworthy, brushing this sop aside, demanded whether this meant, in effect, the end of Dewar's and Daniel's career. Mr Bridgeman denied that it did. Kenworthy pointed out how easy it was going to be for Their Lordships to block Dewar's promotion, simply by seeing that he got no opportunity to complete the five months or so of sea-time he still needed for qualification. He wanted an assurance that this officer would be re-employed quickly, in command of a sea-going ship. But Mr Bridgeman would not commit himself so far. Many captains were in the same position, he said. Dewar must take his chance.

No sooner was this passage ended than Bellairs clamoured for a Blue Book on the affair. The request was turned down. Kenworthy returned to raise another needling issue: who had been responsible for foisting additional charges on Commander Daniel at short notice, in contravention of a promise given to Parliament that both officers would be allowed ample time to prepare their defence? Bellairs joined in: it was disgraceful that a court of inquiry should have been staged at a time that gave persons appearing before it only ten minutes in which to collect witnesses.

After this wild flurry, the *Royal Oak* affair tailed off and died away in the last refuge of lost causes and nine-day-wonders, the correspondence columns of *Times*, *Morning Post* and *Daily Telegraph*. An occasional flash from a retired admiral in a distant part of the world kept it spasmodically flaring up – a protest, as a rule, against ' certain M.P.s ' who refused to give the Admiralty credit for being able to look

ADMIRAL OF THE FLEET SIR ROGER KEYES
(*later* LORD KEYES OF ZEEBRUGGE AND DOVER)

after its own affairs. From the French Riviera, where some of Admiral Keyes's ships had arrived, a gossip columnist reported:

'Never has the British Navy been so commented on before, in every port from St Raphael to Monaco. The reason? The courts martial, of course. . . . Officers and ratings are frozenly mute over recent happenings. The order apparently is to smile – and discuss the *mistral*. The marines have come in for a good deal of chaff, of the " Now they can't go and tell it to the marines any more " order.'

The three officers were home again. They returned to another freak spell of wintry weather, and hail, snow and sleet drove across the south coast of England when they landed. Admiral Collard came to Southampton in the *Otranto*. He gave reporters his now-famous shaggy-browed glare, said " I am sorry to disappoint you but I have nothing to say," stepped into a waiting car and left at once for his home in Surrey. Cars were waiting also for Dewar and Daniel and their wives at the King George V dock in London, where their ship, the *Ranpura*, docked the same day. A large crowd had assembled to watch them disembark, and when a couple of hundred stevedores all downed tools together and surrounded Dewar's car, cheering him, it began almost to have the look of a planned demonstration.

Exactly six months later, all who had knowledgeably wagered that the Admiralty would kick Dewar and Daniel out as surely, if not quite as publicly, as they had kicked Collard, lost their bets. Captain Dewar's name was among the new appointments to H.M. ships – and in command.

She was the *Tiger*, a vintage battle-cruiser, based on Portsmouth, running trials and doing experimental firings for the gunnery school at Whale Island. In her, and in her successor, H.M.S. *Iron Duke*, the Captain saw out the evening of his naval career. In the former Grand fleet flagship he took classes of British, Canadian and Australian sub-lieutenants to sea, young men hoping to specialise as gunnery officers, at the stage he had been at so long before, when he laid down the law to Captain Percy Scott and was advised ' never to put in writing over your signature anything that might be construed into presumption or . . . twisted into conflict with the regulations '. He stood where his ancient stumbling-block, Jellicoe, had stood to deploy the battleships in a ' rigid single line ' at Jutland; and he operated under a more recent stumbling-block, Keyes, who was now Commander-in-Chief at Portsmouth. The papers mentioned both officers among the forthcoming attractions at Portsmouth's Navy Week in August 1929. But Dewar was gone by then: awarded the customary consolation prizes of an appointment as A.D.C. to the King, a ' good service ' pension of £150 a year and promotion to rear-admiral, and immediately placed upon the retired list. He had not hoisted, and never would hoist, his admiral's flag.

He was fifty, his only regret at leaving the Navy ' an unfulfilled ambition to exercise some influence on the education and training of junior officers '; and a career to which his talents, as some thought, were better suited, looked like beginning soon. He went in 1930, just after the London Naval Conference ended, to the House of Commons to address the Parliamentary Labour party about it – outlining the argument for a reduction in capital ship strength. At the general election of 1931 he fought Portsmouth North as a Socialist and a Fabian.

His opponent, Sir B. Falle, was coming up for his twenty-first year in the constituency, and Dewar was considered to have done well to poll more than a third of the votes in a straight fight. He might have done better, but for a scurrilous poster put out under his name. Billed as an issue of 'Admiral Dewar's Election News', it depicted the ex-Kaiser and Mr (later Sir) Montagu Norman, the governor of the Bank of England, under a headline: 'Leaders of Lost Causes'. The caption said, 'In 1916 the British Navy beat the Kaiser at Jutland – in 1931 the British Navy beat Montagu Norman at Invergordon'. The text identified the military aims of the one with the monetary policy of the other, as joint wreckers of working-class homes. Coming to a naval base, at a date when the Invergordon mutiny was less than a month old and the Navy was still extremely sensitive about it, this publication must have lost Dewar some votes. He told the press while he was canvassing that it was 'just a propaganda sheet . . . in no way seditious or libellous . . . the Tory party issues the same kind of thing . . . the sheet merely states facts'. But before the contest was over he spoke more sadly, more wisely and with more disillusionment:

'I beg to state that I had absolutely nothing to do with its design and had never seen it . . . perhaps I was remiss in not exercising more efficient supervision. . . . I deeply regret that this picture should have been associated with my name.' Next time he would be more careful.

There was no next time. The Conservative candidate at the 1935 general election was a sailor and a new boy to politics too: of all people, Admiral Sir Roger Keyes. He went in with a sweeping majority. But Dewar was not opposing his old Commander-in-Chief and the Portsmouth North electorate was denied the fascinating spectacle of two admirals, whose paths – and swords – had so often crossed before, fighting out on the hustings the campaigns of the Dardanelles and of Grand Harbour, Valletta.

That Dewar had not forgotten his crusade for a smaller, streamlined Navy was shown in the report of a speech he made at the opening of a photographic exhibition at the Ilford galleries in London. Indicating the impressive shots of the *Rodney* and the *Nelson* at high speed on the wall behind him, he told his audience of art-lovers and camera enthusiasts that ships a quarter the size of these could do the job they did, better and at a fraction of the cost. The Government's attitude to the question of aerial bombardment, he said, illustrated a point he wanted to make. The nation had strenuously resisted a practical disarmament proposal at Geneva (the Hoover plan, more respected by posterity than it was in 1934) in order to preserve its right to drop bombs on the villages of the Pathans and Afridis. He hoped the policy that was apparently so good for tribesmen in time of peace would not turn out to be too bad for Britain in time of war, although London was a rather easier target than a native settlement on the North-West frontier.

But his chairman, a retired colonel, was more in touch with the spirit of the age. He must take issue with the Vice-Admiral (Dewar had been promoted on the retired list in the normal way), he said, having spent the past twenty-five years in and around the Khyber Pass. He assured his audience that Pathans who had been bombed out of their homes by the Royal Air Force were ever afterwards ' on the best of terms with the British and each other '.

Dewar's book – a big one – ' The Navy from Within ', came out in 1939. Part *apologia pro vita sua* and part a critical appreciation of the naval training system with post-mortems on Jutland and the Dardanelles and the *Royal Oak* affair thrown in, it was coolly received. Experts considered he had spoiled a reasonable case by overstating it: ' It will need a better-drawn indictment than Admiral Dewar's to convince readers that the shortcomings disclosed in his own story of thirty-eight years in the Royal Navy were one and all on the Navy's side and none on the side of the narrator '. In spite of being a little ' chip-on-the-shoulder ' in places, the book was pleasingly written and provided an instructive short course in ' independent thought '. For all that its author disclaimed ' any personal feelings ' about the *Royal Oak* affair, it revealed how the wounds still ached.

True to form, Dewar took cudgels to his reviewers. ' More concerned with the author than the contents ', he found them; and they had missed the point of his arguments about old campaigns and credited him with holding opinions he had not expressed. But all of a sudden Gallipoli and Jutland sounded old-fashioned; for the second World War had begun and the Vice-Admiral was at the head of the correspondence columns with some commonsense questions about Air Raid Precautions.

' Hundreds of thousands of men and women are " standing by " all over Great Britain for air raids,' he began, in a letter to *The Times*, ' and being paid £2 to £3 a week for it. Is this large expenditure of money and manpower justified ? '

Why, he asked in another, must country-dwellers suffer

the danger and inconvenience of driving about without lights? Would a car's headlamps on a rural road be so helpful to the enemy? 'After all, bombs must be dropped somewhere and what better place for them than the fields and ditches alongside our country roads?' The letter appeared adjoining the property advertisements, column after column of items headed 'ARP – secluded country retreat', 'ARP – scheduled safe area' and so forth. Like so much of the common sense and logic Dewar had been noted for all his career, it was unpalatable in the context.

In 1940, Kenneth Gilbert Balmain Dewar went back to the Admiralty to do his war service. He was almost sixty. He worked in the Historical Section of the Training and Staff Duties Division, of which his older brother, Captain A. C. Dewar, R.N. (Retd.),was now the head. There is something poignant in the picture of this elderly admiral, himself a piece of history, studying at his desk in Whitehall the histories of forgotten men and campaigns, while history of a violent and up-to-date kind is made over his head in the London skies.

After the war ended, Vice-Admiral Dewar lived in retirement in a suburb of Worthing, Sussex. From time to time he wrote to the press, applying the lessons of history to the modern Navy's problems. The protection of shipping in the next war, the combing out of inessential services, a 'first-things-first' approach to the nuclear fleet question, were among his themes. His last word on 'tactical paralysis' — a big *critique* entitled 'Jutland to Singapore' — was unfinished when he died, aged eighty-four, in September 1964. Of the numerous officers of 'high professional competence' who were broken one way or another in the *Royal Oak* affair, he was the last survivor.

Boys used to run away to sea and never be heard of again. Rear-Admiral Collard came home from sea and was scarcely heard of again. The car that took him to Surrey from the s.s. *Otranto* on Easter Saturday 1928 took him out of public life and away from the Royal Navy for ever. Like Dewar, he was promoted vice-admiral on the retired list in due course. Like Dewar, he received no official honours after retirement, although at the time of the affair he was almost qualified for a more-or-less routine knighthood. Like Dewar he wrote a book.

But Collard's book was 'A Textbook of Netting', a modest little wartime production, born of austere make-do-and-mend propaganda, explaining how to turn lengths of string and rope into shopping-baskets and tennis-nets. The frontispiece was a snapshot of the now ageing admiral, a gruff and gimlet-eyed country squire, demonstrating netting techniques in his study. From the portrait, or the text, one would never know the author had naval connections; except that a picture on the study wall is referred to as that of H.M.S. *Active*, the last full-rigged naval vessel to leave Portsmouth harbour under sail.

With the outbreak of World War Two, an opportunity came for Admiral Collard to renew the naval connection. He declined it. He became a part-time member of the Observer Corps and, as his daughter recalls, 'took a tremendous pride in doing this job really well' – which would surprise no one who knew him. Once a week throughout those years he went over to the Byculla School at Langley in Sussex (he was living at Rake, near Petersfield), to teach the girls household maintenance – not only the construction of string shopping-nets, but also elementary plumbing,

decorating and electrics. Collard had always, rather un-
characteristically for a life-loving seadog of old England,
been an instructor of infinite skill and patience; in his
voluntary job at the girls' school he was as happy as ever he
had been in his life. And his visits are said to have been a
bright spot in the timetable for all his pupils.

After his wife died, Bernard St George Collard went to
spend his last years at a small hotel in Sherborne, Dorset –
he had a family connection with the well-known public
school. He might have been seen most days in the season, a
calm, contemplative old man, fishing the salmon streams of
the county. His social life was limited to an occasional visit
from, or to, a relative or an old friend. He had returned to
his native region almost as a stranger, and was known in the
country districts as a shy visitor is known – by sight and no
more; as one who courteously accepts conversation when
it is forced on him, but never seeks it of his own accord.

Collard's name and Dewar's, bracketed together so many
times in the press in the spring of 1928, were bracketed
again, and for the last time, on Friday the 13th April 1962.
On the correspondence page of *The Times* appeared, as its
principal letter of the day, a warning to the Government by
Admiral Dewar regarding the proposal to spend twenty
million pounds on a Polaris submarine. Opposite, Admiral
Collard's death was announced, at the age of eighty-six.

He was recalled to readers as ' the principal figure in the
most notable courts martial in the Royal Navy for many
years '. His obituarist, after paying a tribute to his personal
courage as a young officer (in saving life at sea) and a captain
commanding a ship in action, came down at last firmly on
his side in the notorious affair:

'Complaints which he had a right to make were not received with that spirit of unquestioning loyalty usually associated with the Service. . . . The affair was badly handled . . . but, for this, Collard was not to blame. His conduct throughout was straightforward, frank and open, and he had many sympathisers among his brother officers at this unhappy termination of his career. He bore the calamity manfully and without complaint. It was but one side of the character of this blunt and outspoken sailor which was shown in the court martial proceedings.'

There were not many mourners at his funeral and only one or two sailors, colleagues from his earliest days at sea. Collard's rise and fall had elements of classical tragedy about it, not quite the tragedy of the man of power and authority whom the gods bring down for arrogance, but of him of whom Seferis writes, in connection with another career worn and withered in its prime:

'His friends were few. He was difficult in every way.
The time arrived and he was torn to pieces by dogs.'

On the 23rd April 1928, the tenth anniversary of the battle of Zeebrugge, when the news pages of the *Daily Mail* announced the final destruction by earthquake of the city of Corinth and the wreck of Miss Dolores del Rio's third marriage and the promotion, from lieutenant to lieutenant-commander, of Lord Louis Mountbatten, the following letter appeared in its correspondence columns; one of several on the same theme:

'Sir,

'May I congratulate Commander Daniel and your newspaper on his joining your staff? There has been a

233

strong public feeling that the services of so brilliant and courageous an officer should not be lost to the nation.'

The Socialist press in general, throughout the affair, had taken Dewar for its hero; the *Daily Mail* had made an especial favourite of Daniel. And, as soon as he disclosed his intention of retiring (explaining that he still loved the Navy, but that he had no illusions about the effect of a black mark at this critical stage of his career, and was not prepared to 'soldier on' in dead-end jobs for the rest of his life), it invited him to become a member of its literary staff; reminding readers, in case they had not heard about them already, of the Commander's obvious qualifications for the job. He had in his time been both author and publisher (of ' H.M. Valiants ') and was still the owner of the original Daniel Press, which his uncle Henry had founded at Worcester College, Oxford, along with William Morris, to establish a renaissance of illuminated lettering and ' artistic ' printing and to produce collectors' pieces of books in strictly limited editions, on hand-made paper and lavishly decorated. The Commander's short history of all the ships named H.M.S. *Valiant* was a work of this type.

That same week the newly appointed journalist had his own by-line in the *Daily Mail*, with a facetiously written sketch describing his arrival at Northcliffe House to report for duty in ' Come-aboard-to-join-sir-please ' style.

In a highly flattering (and by no means inaccurate or undeserved) tribute to his accomplishments and character, the *Daily Mail* threw out a hint that Commander Daniel's special talent for organising might be employed in some worthwhile publicity stunt, in which he himself could participate; it was recalled that he had once earned ' fame ' among his ' brother officers ' by walking from Portsmouth to London – seventy-two miles – in under twenty-four hours, to win a bet of a hundred pounds.

But when the manufacturers of a popular fountain-pen cashed in on Daniel's ' fame ' by borrowing the sword he had taken to his court martial and making it the centrepiece of a display in a Piccadilly shop window, captioned with the obvious slogan, his ' brother officers ', the world over, were shocked; and a raiding party of sub-lieutenants undergoing courses at the Royal Naval College at Greenwich either removed it forcibly (as some reports had it) or persuaded the management to take it out.

One contemporary has said of Daniel, *à propos* the advertising slogan, that ' *his* pen was not very mighty '. He nevertheless became a useful and well-known ' nautical ' correspondent, as it was then called, for the Northcliffe press, and scored a valuable success when he took the *Daily Mail* yacht, the *Wild Duck*, round some of the south coast seaside resorts on a circulation-building voyage during the summer of 1930.

Daniel's resignation from the staff of that newspaper one year later made no headlines. His name, indeed, meant little to the reading public any more. Casual acquaintances showed surprise – it had been a plum job, in some ways, exceptionally well-paid. But close friends had expected it; a man, they said, of Daniel's training and background, of his strictly principled, not to say puritanical, outlook, could never have survived in Fleet Street for long – except, possibly, as his own boss. That, in fact, was what he was about to try: freelance journalism. It did not suffice to maintain him and his family in anything like the style to which they had become accustomed; small commissions for the sailing and yachting press failed to answer; and a novel – a romance with a nautical background – on which he had pinned great hopes never found a publisher. An old colleague, meeting him one day in the streets of Portsmouth at this period, said he looked ' a sad, rather neglected figure ', in the same smart blue suit and red-spotted tie he had worn to travel to his court martial. A fish too long out of water; or, as a relative more accurately expresses it, ' a man of whose ambition the mainspring had snapped '.

Stony, harsh and beset with injustices as Daniel had felt the long path to naval distinction to have been, that of life ashore was stonier still, and split with many turnings. Throughout the nineteen-thirties he moved from job to job – not that he had become disgruntled, or a drifter, but because some unforeseen contingency, time and again, upset his plans and his prospects. Daniel these days was more of an idealist than ever, deeply concerned with service to the community. Fringe enthusiasms embraced freemasonry, scoutmastering (he was a district commissioner in Surrey), and youth leadership of various kinds; not to mention his old spiritual inclinations for Christian Science.

To such a person, the post to which he was appointed in 1932 seemed perfectly suited: manager and secretary of World Explorers, Limited. The firm, which operated from an office on Charing Cross pier in London, existed, not as its he-mannish-sounding title led one to expect, to explore romantic territories in the unknown places of the earth, but to arrange goodwill visits for students and young people between Britain and the Continental countries – mainly Germany, unfortunately for its administration, and World Explorers did not long survive the withdrawal, early in the Nazi era, of the support it largely depended on.

Daniel moved to another vocational job, that of appeals secretary for the National Institute for the Blind. His conscientiousness and devotion to duty were rewarded after two years with promotion to the general secretaryship of St Dunstan's, the hospital for war-blinded members of the Forces, under the then Captain Sir Ian Fraser. He was doing equally promisingly in this position and seemed at last to have overcome the disappointments and disenchantments of the past decade – when his health broke down.

It was 1938. Daniel, in his late forties, was from now onwards to battle against both periodic illness and a succession of strokes of malignant fortune such as few figures already handicapped by the stigma of past notoriety can have been called on to withstand. In this year his life entered a phase of Zolaesque tragedy. His marriage failed. His home – a picturesque thatched, timber cottage at Purley that he had once affectionately described for *The Times* – was burned to ashes. War found him in the West Country, and he took command of a Home Guard detachment – only a few miles, by coincidence, from Sherborne, where Admiral Collard retired to end his days. It was his temporary salvation.

With the peace, setbacks and disillusionment returned. His health continually deteriorated. He was next heard of in South Africa, working for a shipping company in Port Elizabeth. Obscurely, in August 1955, the once ' capable and smart young officer ', the zealous organiser of lavish shipboard entertainment, the sensitive amateur novelist and playwright, the mercurial gunnery officer of outstanding ability, died there in a city hospital, of arterio-sclerosis, after a year's painful illness.

CHAPTER XIII

The Clouds Roll By

'DEAR Sir Roger,' wrote his old chief of staff, Rear-Admiral Dudley Pound, from Whitehall in mid-May 1928, ' one hears nothing of the *Royal Oak* business now. At first I think people outside the Admiralty were inclined to think it ought to have been hushed up, but later one found . . . the only way to deal with it was drastically and openly.'

A consensus of opinion among surviving senior officers today is not exactly ' inclined to think it ought to have been hushed up ', rather that it ought never to have been allowed to develop. The disrepute into which the Royal Navy was dragged, the impossible position in which the affair placed innocent and courageous officers, the demonstration of the Sea Lords' lack of touch with personnel afloat and of guts to stand up to the politicians – these memories still rankle and many a retired captain and admiral still shudders slightly at the merest mention of the case. ' Miserably handled ' is posterity's verdict, whatever the rights and wrongs of individual attitudes.

Admiral Keyes, about to hand over the Mediterranean fleet to Sir Frederick Field, for whom he cared little, read into Pound's letter something approaching full and final exoneration from blame in the affair. ' One hears nothing of the *Royal Oak* business now ' – it was consoling news for Sir Roger, his long and arduous tour of duty brilliantly and memorably executed, sailing home with his family and his string of ponies, to await the outcome of a slow reshuffle of appointments in the Home commands that would leave the First Sea Lord's chair vacant.

But from the time he arrived in London he seemed to be hearing about little *but* the *Royal Oak* business. If the Admiralty had been out of touch with the feelings of personnel afloat, Keyes was even less *au fait* with the shift of the nation's emotions about its proudest institution. Jealous admiration for the Navy was clouded with disgust, reverence for senior officers corrupted into ridicule, and in Service and non-Service circles alike there was cynical talk of the ' Admirals' trade union '. The most alarming shock came when he paid on the First Sea Lord the formal call that every admiral pays on relinquishing a command.

' Madden told me the King was very angry with me about the conduct of the *Royal Oak* case ! ' (wrote Keyes in his diary). ' He said he had stayed a night at Windsor and the King would talk about nothing else, continually harking back to the subject ! ! '

' " Not only," Sir Charles Madden said, " would he not accept my assurance that you had done the right thing under the circumstances, but *he* tried to persuade *me* that you were wrong ! " '

Retiring Commanders-in-Chief usually have an audience of the Sovereign. Keyes anxiously awaited his summons, but Madden begged him to avoid the topic at all costs – useless advice to give to the bull-at-a-gate hero of Zeebrugge, even if His Majesty had been minded to let it drop. He marched in on Fullerton, the Naval Secretary, and demanded to know where the King had got all his information from.

And, as he had already vaguely suspected, he found that his own full and final report on the incident had not gone to Buckingham Palace. It was unearthed, and a copy made, and he took it along with him for an audience of about half an hour, during which little else was talked about.

' The King asked me,' says Keyes's journal, ' if there was any precedent in the history of the Navy for one flag-officer hauling down the flag of another. I said I did not know of one.' (The Beresford-Scott incident might have occurred to him.) ' But I still felt I had done the right thing. The King was exceedingly nice to me, but evidently thought I had made a mess of things.'

That was not the only source of the King's displeasure; nor, perhaps, the only reason why the prize for which Sir Roger had been so long in the running – so long out-distancing all competition – was soon to be handed to another. Gossip about the fleet being ' polo crazy ' had come to the royal ear. King George, fanatically jealous of his Navy, never more upset than by ridicule or disparage-ment of it, told the Admiral it was a pity he had encouraged so many young officers to play polo. Keyes stoutly con-tested it. Polo was a training for war, it taught officers to plan and keep fit and get out of their bunks early in the morning . . . made them alert, nimble and brave.

It was not at all the homecoming Keyes had visualised. He privately blamed his successor at Malta for his un-popularity: ' Field did his best to fasten the polo attack on me and I was told by a friend of mine who went out there in a yacht that he used to point out the second polo ground as one of the men's football pitches I had taken from them.'

Keyes felt much better after His Majesty had had a chance

to go over his version of the *Royal Oak* case and Lord Stam-fordham, the Private Secretary, had written a friendly note that his views were 'considerably modified' as a result. Keyes's acknowledgment precipitated a libel action:

'. . . I am glad the King does not think so ill of me as he did. . . . Of course, if I had realised that those two fellows *would make such improper use of their nasty Parliamentary friends* I would not have considered their feelings but would have kept them in other ships until they could have been tried in privacy . . . but I don't think they would have left it at that. . . . I learned afterwards that the night they left Malta they said quite openly that if they were not reinstated or equally well employed every paper in England would ring with their story under big headlines.'

This letter was first published in Brigadier-General Aspinall-Oglander's biography of Roger Keyes, which came out in 1951. Keyes was dead and Daniel abroad, but Dewar very much alive and on the spot, and he instantly sued for libel.

The suit was based on the unfounded suggestion that he had made improper use of friends in Parliament, but there was much, in that part of the book in which Oglander (a family friend of the Keyeses) had loyally done his best to exonerate the former Commander-in-Chief from responsibility for the publicity and scandal of the *Royal Oak* affair, to which Dewar took exception. The book seemed to place all the blame on the courts martial victims, Dewar in particular. For example, in dealing with the night at the House of Commons when the story broke, the author had described Bellairs as having announced that 'the press had received news . . . that the officers of the *Royal Oak* had refused to sail under Rear-Admiral Collard and had been court-martialled.' What Bellairs actually said was ' Captain and officers ' – in the Royal Navy the word ' officers ' does not include the captain of a ship, who is always referred to separately. This, claimed Dewar, was deliberate distortion. The biographer's omission of the word ' Captain ' was meant to imply – at least to everyone in the Navy – that Dewar was the one who had ' leaked ' the information.

Another misleading sentence included the expression ' eve of sailing ' – that Dewar had made his complaint to Vice-Admiral Kelly ' on the eve of sailing ' for the combined exercises. It had been in fact the court of inquiry that had had to be held at the last moment; Dewar's complaint and Daniel's ' reasons in writing ' were in Collard's hands forty-eight hours earlier.

In the same chapter Brigadier Oglander had excused Keyes's drastic action in removing Rear-Admiral, Captain and Commander, by reference to Dewar's charge that ' the ship's discipline was being undermined '; whereas what the Captain had actually written (and gone on to illustrate with a description of the three incidents) was that Rear-Admiral Collard's behaviour was ' *calculated* to undermine ' (his position and the general discipline of the ship). Dewar had been especially sensitive on this point: his lasting grievance was against the ' undermining ' allegation. From that kind of talk, he believed, stemmed the talk about which he had known nothing at the time, that he had started the mutiny-and-revolt scare.

Then the book spoke of ' personal friction ' between Collard and his flag-captain, in a manner designed to give an impression that the faults were all on the latter's side;

and that all the incidents were ' so petty in themselves as to be shamingly ridiculous ' – implying that Dewar was a frivolous or mischievous complainer. According to him, in short, Brigadier Oglander had displayed bias in favour of the admirals in his account of the *Royal Oak* affair.

The subject of the ex-Captain's Statement of Claim before the courts relied mainly on the quotation of the correspondence between Admiral Keyes and the King's Private Secretary, in particular the phrase ' improper use of their nasty Parliamentary friends '. The words were taken to mean that Dewar and Daniel had made false or misleading statements to the press and to members of Parliament as soon as they arrived in England, to the effect that a mutiny or a revolt had occurred, or was brewing, in the Mediterranean fleet; that the *Royal Oak's* officers, as Bellairs told the House, had refused to sail under Rear-Admiral Collard and had been court-martialled; that Dewar and Daniel had talked from personal or improper motives, to secure reinstatement or some professional advantage, knowing quite well the statements were untrue; that they had been guilty of conduct entirely contrary to their duty and the traditions and code of honour of the Royal Navy. Vice-Admiral Dewar now demanded damages and the removal of the passages he complained of in future copies of the book.

In July 1953 the defendants in the libel action apologised in the High Court and the record was withdrawn. At last it was acknowledged, officially, that Dewar had no part whatever in spreading the false rumours that had rebounded in banner captions in the popular press in March 1928; that he had made no communications to the papers at that time, or to Parliamentary friends, nice or nasty; and that other allegations were unfounded. He accepted the apology, and costs, and a substantial sum in satisfaction of his claim for damages.

This was all in the undreamed-of future, a generation and another World War away. In the summer of 1928, the *Royal Oak* affair was dead for most people already, only Admiral Sir Roger Keyes vigorously puffing at cold embers, determined to see that everyone got the facts right before another earthquake supervened. He took time off to attend the first-ever inter-Services polo match, Royal Navy *versus* the Royal Air Force, but throughout the Parliamentary recess, on golf course and grouse moor and country estate, he busily lobbied the politicians, especially those who had been critical of his action. From one who had made no attempt to conceal his disgust, Philip Cunliffe-Lister (the President of the Board of Trade), he drew the admission: 'If all those concerned had dealt as decently by you as you did by them, we shouldn't have had the trouble.'

In the autumn the First Lord of the Admiralty invited Sir Roger to become Commander-in-Chief at Portsmouth – most important of the Home commands, one of the proudest and most senior positions in the Navy; but, unlike his last job, offering little to an admiral alive with ambition. Few had ever gone from this appointment to become First Sea Lord. But a general election was pending and anything might happen. "Take it," said Beatty, and Keyes took it.

From Admiralty House at Portsmouth, the new Commander-in-Chief set himself to win over the members of Ramsay Macdonald's new Government. Lord Beatty promised to put in a good word with the Prime Minister, Keyes himself made friends with A. V. Alexander, the new

First Lord. It was no use. Sir Frederick Field, a colourless person beside himself, had been promised the post. Friends offered the consolation that Keyes was too outspoken ever to be the First Sea Lord, too mindful of the Navy's prestige and too influential in the fleet. Another big naval conference was coming off, the Government of the day more anxious than the last to strip Britain of her few remaining warships. Keyes would never be a party to their decisions, they told him, he would resign and carry all the Sea Lords with him. A more realistic appraisal was heard at the tables of some of the captains and admirals in the fleet: ' Thank God for the *Royal Oak* affair. Keyes as First Sea Lord would have been a disaster.'

Keyes entered Parliament in 1935. Still an embarrassingly inarticulate speaker, he brought home to M.P.s the serious-ness of the situation perhaps more effectively than estab-lished orators when he burst out with a cataract of denuncia-tion of the Chamberlain clique and a thinly disguised plug for Churchill as Prime Minister. He fathered the science of Combined Operations (conceived perhaps at that distant date, 1927, when he had approved the *Royal Oak's* landing party orders for Dragamesti as ' the best thing she had done on the station '), and perhaps this organisational triumph was *his* most memorable contribution to the history of arms. But he was a classic type by the time the war got into its stride: the embodiment of that mythical symbol, the king whose reign is over but who will not die. Not too old, but too senior.

He pestered Churchill with obsessive requests to be allowed to lead a charge somewhere, in Taku Forts or Zeebrugge fashion. Frustrated, he was prevailed on to second a censure motion on the Government, condemning its conduct of the war. Removed to the House of Lords, he committed a solecism by intervening in a debate on the day of his introduction (like many a hopeless public speaker, Keyes found the temptation to say his piece irresistible). On a tour of Australia and New Zealand he showed that a voyage to the Antipodes was not long enough to keep him out of the British public eye: he made new headlines and dismayed his hosts by shoving in an oar in a local labour dispute.

Keyes – Admiral of the Fleet Lord Keyes, he had ended as – died in 1945. The nation was astonished to hear that he was barely seventy years old. He had held high rank when the current military leaders had been schoolboys and subalterns and midshipmen. Though the bright image was tarnished a little towards the close, his passing seemed to most people like the passing of a great patriarchal figure from the Age of Heroes.

In a sense, his life had ended when he relinquished the Mediterranean command in 1928; when, for his epitaph, he could have borrowed Darius the Persian's: 'I was a friend to my friends. As a warrior I vanquished all. As a hunter I prevailed. I could do everything.'

Up to the *Royal Oak* affair, the Navy had rarely been known to throw open the shutters and admit outsiders to an intimate glimpse of its domestic tiffs and tensions. The theory that the public had a right to see what its taxes were being spent on was less popular then than it later became. In the *Royal Oak* courts martial the window had been lit full beam, to disclose an exceptionally personal scene, to reveal how the stiff and unapproachable heroes of bridge and quarter-deck (mysterious figures even to the sailors they commanded) were, after all, creatures of flesh and blood and emotion, just like normal human beings.

Primed by the nation's reaction to this discovery, some sections of the press kept a curious watch on the activities of the Silent Service, on both upper and lower deck. The life of the fleet, it turned out, was not exclusively a matter of cocktail parties on the Riviera, or football at the United Services ground, or pig-sticking in the Maldives. And humble bluejackets, it seemed, sometimes had opinions of their own, when subjects other than the rival merits of Malta's Egyptian Queen and Sunrise Bar were in dispute; these opinions could be elicited, by gentlemen of the press for instance, who understood the naval rating's psychology and had learned to handle him a little more judiciously than those who descended on Gibraltar in the spring of 1928.

The published expression of sailors' privately held views on the Naval Discipline Act was said to have achieved much of what Bellairs and Kenworthy campaigned for unsuccessfully in the House of Commons. (Dewar claimed that the *Royal Oak* scandal was the cause of the alteration allowing appeals to the High Court against naval courts martial decisions.)

One newspaper, it was said, started to monitor radio transmissions in the fleet. Whether excited by this surveillance, or unsettled by irresponsible comment after the affair, or only conforming to a general social movement of the age, sailors were caught in disturbing scenes of insubordination in the nineteen-thirties rather more frequently than they had been in the past; and it was significant that ships formerly attached to the First Battle Squadron of 1928 were often involved. The *Revenge* appeared as a ' mutiny ship ' – for one day – in 1930; the *Warspite* in 1937; and in between came the *Lucia* affair and the real drama of Invergordon (several ex-Mediterranean battleships concerned here) in 1931.

Collard, Dewar and Daniel: the affair destroyed all three's hopes of high command. To Keyes it brought the one great disappointment of an otherwise brilliant career. In the list of those who helped to make a legend in Hangar ' A ' on board the *Eagle* at Gibraltar that spring, only Paymaster Captain Measham, the Deputy Judge Advocate, appeared to reap a quick benefit. He was not long in being made a paymaster rear-admiral.

Later on, the Bandmaster's was a modest success story. Percy Edward Barnacle, had he been able to get home when the trials ended, would have found himself famous. His name was a gift to comedians. He was portrayed in the Adelphi revue, *Many Happy Returns*, that summer; in a sketch called *Moments with the Really Great*, and in a popular song. Guests on board the *Royal Oak* at functions where the band played regarded him with a frank curiosity which he took gracefully and came quietly to enjoy. Ashore at Malta he was pointed out as one of the Navy's ' characters '.

He stayed in the ship for about a year after the affair, then returned to his depot at Portsmouth to complete time for pension. Name and fame as much as professional ability earned him the job of conductor with the celebrated Betteshanger Colliery band when he retired. He is today comfortably settled in Deal, an old marine school-of-music stronghold, where bandsmen recruits look on him as their grandfathers may have looked on some veteran man-of-Kent from Waterloo. For Percy Edward Barnacle, being sworn at by the Admiral had its compensations. And he is now the only veteran of the affair who is still alive.

Another who emerged unscathed was Vice-Admiral John Donald Kelly. It was not the first time he had marched safely across thin ice and seen his colleagues, cautiously tiptoeing, go in all around him: something of the same kind had happened when the German sailors scuttled their ships – an accomplishment that Kelly, as Director of the Operations Division, had been there to prevent. Relieved as second-in-command, Mediterranean fleet, by his brother Howard, he became Admiral Commanding Reserves, and was on the point of retirement when the Invergordon mutiny broke out. Kelly was asked to take over the Home fleet, and thus fell heir to the post, titles and honours of one of the innocent victims. He died an Admiral of the Fleet in 1936.

Invergordon was no salvation for Rear-Admiral Tomkinson, the former Chief of Staff at Malta, who was unlucky actually to be serving in the Home fleet at the time. Along with those of most of the senior officers on the spot, his head rolled before even his friend Keyes could put in a good word – at a time, indeed, when Keyes's advocacy might have been more a hindrance than a help.

Of the numerous wardroom officers in the *Royal Oak* whose ' guts in coming forward ' Dewar held to be about the only redeeming feature of the whole business, few made marks of prominence in their subsequent careers. It was a period of large-scale reductions in strength and axings of personnel, admittedly; but the younger men who survived

the naval depression (and these, by virtue of their appointments to a crack battleship of the Mediterranean fleet, must
already have given some proof that they were better qualified
to than most) might have been expected to reach distinguished rank in the second World War. One at least – and
he one of the most forthright in his championship of captain
and commander – emerged without a black mark against
his name. This was G. E. M. O'Donnell, the *Royal Oak's*
gunnery officer, who entered the war of 1939-45 as a post-
captain and naval attaché in Ankara.

Others left the Service before the war. Brownlow was
one, and another was Crichton, the captain's secretary, who
retired in 1935. Some were not long outside when the
national emergency drew them back: like Harry Goulding
the chaplain, who returned to serve throughout at an air
station. Claude Attwood, the fiery major of marines, whose
animosity towards the admiral was so marked at the witness
stand, retired very soon after the affair. A forgotten man,
he re-entered the Corps in 1940, to hold down a forgotten
job – the incongruous one, for a marine, of Sea Transport
Officer at Barrow-in-Furness. There could have been
scarcely any appointment less ardently competed for, one
imagines, unless it were that of piermaster at Wigan. Still
on the retired list in 1964, Claude Attwood was still a major
of marines, a rank he attained at an unusually early age and
one he had held for forty years.

One of the stenographers who assisted Captain Measham
at the courts martial eventually reached commissioned rank
and retired as a warrant writer. Another, Writer Surrey,
went down in H.M.S. *Hood* in 1941.

What of the politicians whose preoccupation with the

Royal Oak affair made it the most alarming, amusing, disgraceful, consoling and enlightening (depending on which angle you viewed it from) news story of the year? Carlyon Bellairs and Kenworthy both lost their seats in the 1931 general election. The former, the Conservative of radical opinions, declined a baronetcy in accordance with his often-expressed conviction that political honours corrupted and should be abolished. The latter, a Socialist of aristocratic background, succeeded to the ancient title of Lord Strabolgi in 1934.

Bellairs took no further active part in politics after the National Government came into power. He was a man of broad rather than deep intellect, and his interests covered a wide area of public life: he continued to pamphleteer and lecture on a variety of subjects. In Richmond's time, he was a frequent visitor to the naval War College and to the Imperial Defence College. Bellairs was a wealthy man, and he married more money. After his wife's death he applied part of the fortune to the setting up of a unique memorial to her: a biological research institute in the West Indies. Living for the most part in and around Barbados, Commander Bellairs found himself before his death in 1955 a not-too-distant neighbour of Mr C. Day Kimball, the barrister cousin of Commander Daniel. An American by birth (Daniel's mother had been a native of the United States), Kimball could never, in looks or speech or manner, be mistaken for anything else, but he was in fact a natural-ised British subject at the time of the courts martial; and he ended a fairly distinguished career at the Bar in the position of a *puisne* Judge in Bermuda – where he died in 1960.

Lieutenant-Commander the Honourable Joseph Kenworthy, M.P., returned to politics when the death of his
father gave him a title and entry into the House of Lords.
The peers found him as entertaining, garrulous and provoca-
tive as the commoners had done and for four historic years,
from the Munich crisis to the fall of Tobruk, he was Opposition chief whip. Lord Strabolgi, as he now became,
served as a lieutenant in the Home Guard and wrote a book
about the war in the Mediterranean, in which he clamoured
opportunistically for a 'sea-change' in the British and
American conceptions of naval command and strategy,
before the Allies ventured to take on Japan. He died in 1953.

William Clive Bridgeman, First Lord of the Admiralty in
1928, yielded to Mr A. V. Alexander in 1929. Created a
viscount, he looked forward, not back, and solidified,
predictably, into a pillar of the Establishment. He was
elected president of the M.C.C. in 1931, became a governor
of the B.B.C. in 1933 and its Chairman in 1935 – holding
this appointment for only a few weeks before he died.
Lord Bridgeman had filled posts of high distinction and
influence in his time – he had been Home Secretary in two
administrations before he went to the Admiralty – but he
could hardly be said to have made a lasting mark in any job.
He seemed rather to have been elevated by accident to each
position, happy to plod along in the footsteps of his pre-
decessors, to keep the pot boiling for his successors; sometimes he kept it boiling so long that the contents appeared to
have evaporated away.

CHAPTER XIV

Sunset at Malta

DARKNESS falls quickly over Malta on a spring evening. Scarcely has the ' Alert' sounded and the sunset call echoed off the bastions, and the moored ships exchanged jack and ensign for bow and stern lights, than the stars are shining above Grand Harbour. All round the inlets the waterfront is a string of lights. Past the entrance, not visible from most parts of the anchorage, the pencil beam of St Elmo's light whirls round, mainly for the benefit of trans-Mediterranean shipping, for only infrequently nowadays does a warship or trooper come in and out after dark, unless the N.A.T.O. fleet or the American squadron is about.

No great battleships lumber up to their berths these days, few white-ensign ships nose through to the cruiser moorings. If someone re-allocates a selection of buoys without telling everyone else, any warships that may have entered in the wrong order have ample manoeuvring room to change places.

The lights go up along the Fishmarket and the Marina; the arc-lamps on the crane-heads at Parlatorio wharf beat down on the sandstone tunnels and dry-docks like a mid-day sun. There is floodlighting up on the heights too, on the façades of the big new tourist hotels in Floriana and Sliema and the yellow domes of churches in Senglea, Vittoriosa and Cospicua, the ancient three cities. The jangle of bells competes a while with the mounting roar of evening traffic, surrenders to it and dies down. The nightly parade of young folk begins along Strada Reale (Kingsway, they call it now): not so dense a throng as it used to be and nearly all of them Maltese, many with an ear cocked for a political broadcast blaring out of a loudspeaker in a van or a party office – though many, too, will be at home watching television. An occasional knot of sailors, quite an eye-catching sight these days (and it is less than an even chance that they are wearing 'H.M.S.' cap ribbons), clusters at the Indian carpet shop or the lace retailer or the filigree merchant or, down the 'Gut', haggles at the entrance to a dive.

On upper and lower Baraccas (names with comical associations once, descriptive of the *embonpoint* of the ladies of the chorus in the Malta opera, but the allusion is lost on the modern sailor) older citizens saunter and stand and look down on the night-blue water. Little stirs afloat. If they wait long enough they may see a dghaisa lurching out to the solitary British cruiser, with a couple of ladies in dinner dress and an officer with gold-braided cap and boat-cloak of blue cloth, lined with white with gold chain and lion-head fastening at the throat: a rare cameo, growing rarer, a glimpse of the glorious epoch of summer ball and tea dance, dinner party and admiral's reception, in the great days of the great ships.

Most of the dghaisamen watch and wait, or sleep, cradled in their boats on the silent surface of the harbour. Some have come ashore for the night already and are tying up their craft to the wall on Customs House steps, that con-gested needle's-eye of shops, offices and waterfront *impedi-*

menta that every new arrival to the island must pass through
– and which a rise of six inches in the level of the Mediterranean sea would inundate.

As the dghaisamen lower their lanterns one by one from
sternpost and beaky prow, a tourist idling on the jetty can
make out the boat's badge, entwined in the intricate scrollwork of her sides: an admiral's red-cross flag with red discs
on the white and near it, up by the bow, the name *Royal
Oak*. Alongside her lies *Queen Elizabeth*, just along the
jetty *Revenge*. A few minutes more, and he will see *Warspite, Royal Sovereign, Malaya* and some others come in.
Names like these help to date the dghaisas. These flimsy
rowboats will be forty years old, or thereabouts. They will
have gone into the water about the time Sir Roger Keyes
first hoisted his flag above the ramparts and chose his
flagship. They have listened once to Battle Squadron
'shop' in times of crisis and polo conversation by the hour,
and they too have had their *Moments with the Really Great*.
Today, in Grand Harbour, they are the last positive link
with all that the words 'Mediterranean Fleet' stood for in
the years between the wars. The glory and the grandeur
have gone, and the dghaisas remain.

One of the chief participants in the *Royal Oak* affair is left
unaccounted for: the 'Mighty *Oak*' herself.

Until the outbreak of war in 1939 she journeyed between
home waters and the Mediterranean, underwent the modernisation of her class and was often a flagship again. In the
months following the removal of Collard, Dewar and
Daniel she triumphantly vindicated her reputation in the
eyes of the fleet by carrying off the Battle Squadron gunnery

trophy and doing better than she had ever done before in
the annual regatta, failing by only one point in a never-to-
be-forgotten last race to take the cup from the fleet flagship.
But achievements such as these have to be worked up for
over a long period and the credit would have gone to
Wake-Walker as well as Daniel and his successors, to other
captains besides Dewar.

Almost twenty-five years old at the outbreak of the war
in 1939, the *Royal Oak* and her sister ships were becoming
back numbers, but apart from the *Rodney* and *Nelson* and
the untried *King George V* class they were the only battleships Britain had. Low speeds kept them out of the Mediterranean as far as possible and relegated them to Atlantic
convoy work, but H.M.S. *Royal Oak* took no part. She
was the first major casualty of the war, sunk in Scapa Flow
by torpedoes from the submarine U 47 on the night – a
Friday – of 13th October 1939. Eight hundred men lost
their lives in her.

The explosion that wrecked her fostered another mystery.
The stated impossibility of an enemy submarine getting into
the fleet anchorage, the suddenness and completeness of her
destruction, the assurance that survivors smelled no torpedo:
these facts had people whispering ' sabotage ' and wondering
what nebulous influence the affair of 1928 could have
had on the tragedy of 1939. Within four days a German
High Command special bulletin disposed of that line of
speculation:

' Following earlier reports of the sinking of the British
battleship *Royal Oak*, it is now learned that the U-boat
commander, Lieutenant Prien, penetrated the strong de-
fences protecting the anchorage at Scapa Flow and torpedoed

the ship in harbour during the night. The battleship blew up in a few seconds.'

Wolfgang Frank's book, 'Enemy Submarine', made public, from the only eye-witness account, the facts of the *Royal Oak's* last moments. Prien surfaced in the Flow and drew a bead on both *Repulse* and *Royal Oak*, which were silhouetted against the *aurora borealis*; fired a salvo of four torpedoes and then four more. There was a 'shattering explosion' – and nothing more, no response from either ship, no sign of damage. Then came 'a mighty rumbling, crashing, roaring – first, pillars of water, then columns of fire, fragments whirling through the air. . . .' Among these 'fragments' were the after turret that Henry Daniel had once enamelled, the gangway at which the tiny 'commotion' of long ago had taken place, ripped-out fittings that sometimes did duty for a marine bandstand and a brilliantly polished admiral's hatch-cover past which a blunt little flag-officer had once stepped on to the quarter-deck, to stare out across Grand Harbour and digest the contents of a buff envelope full of trouble.